Read 8:

June

Paper – Booksmith

Chestnut H. il

THE
FOUR DAYS OF
MAYAGUEZ

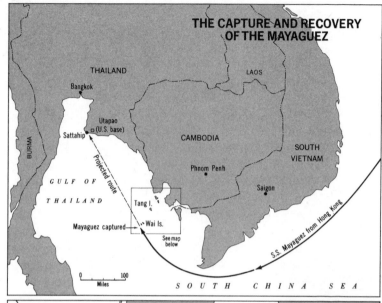

THE CAPTURE AND RECOVERY OF THE MAYAGUEZ

THAILAND

LAOS

Bangkok

Utapao
(U.S. base)

Sattahip

CAMBODIA

SOUTH
VIETNAM

BURMA

GULF OF THAILAND

Phnom Penh

Saigon

Projected route

Tang I.

Wai Is.

Mayaguez captured

See map
below

S.S. Mayaguez from Hong Kong

0   100
Miles

SOUTH   CHINA   SEA

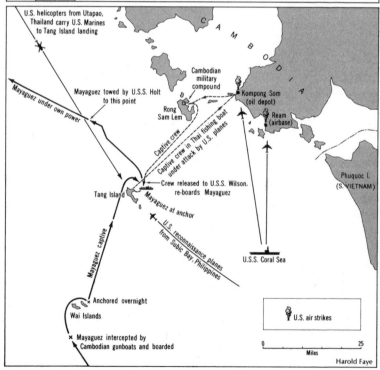

U.S. helicopters from Utapao,
Thailand carry U.S. Marines
to Tang Island landing

C A M B O D I A

Cambodian
military
compound

Mayaguez towed by U.S.S. Holt
to this point

Kompong Som
(oil depot)

Mayaguez under own power

Rong
Sam Lem

Ream
(airbase)

Captive crew

Captive crew in Thai fishing boat
under attack by U.S. planes

Crew released to U.S.S. Wilson.
re-boards Mayaguez

Phuquoc I.
(S. VIETNAM)

Tang Island

Mayaguez at anchor

Mayaguez

U.S. reconnaissance planes
from Subic Bay, Philippines

Mayaguez captive

U.S.S. Coral Sea

Anchored overnight

Wai Islands

Mayaguez intercepted by
Cambodian gunboats and boarded

U.S. air strikes

0   25
Miles

Harold Faye

THE
FOUR DAYS OF
MAYAGUEZ

ROY ROWAN

W · W · NORTON & COMPANY · INC ·

NEW YORK

for
the Men of the *Mayaguez*
and all those
who helped to bring her back
and for
Helen and *her* four men

Contents

Contents

Thursday, May 15

Illustrations

Acknowledgments

Many people made this book possible by sharing their thoughts and memories of the four *Mayaguez* days. I would like to thank President Gerald R. Ford who made time available at the White House for a taping session. Also, David Hume Kennerly, who made his pictures available. I would like to thank the crew of the *Mayaguez* for permitting me to ride with them as a passenger, interviewing and taping along the way. I am especially grateful to Captain Charles T. Miller, master of the *Mayaguez,* who spent tireless hours after his time on the bridge talking into my tape recorder. His only request: that part of the royalties from this book be donated to a fund which he is establishing for the families of those men killed on Koh Tang. I am grateful to Michael R. McEvoy, chairman of Sea-Land Service, Inc. and to his officers for their cooperation; and to Commander J. Michael Rodgers, captain of the U.S.S. *Henry B. Wilson,* Commander Robert A. Peterson, captain of the U.S.S. *Harold E. Holt,* and Commander James A. Messegee, commander U.S. Philippine Air Patrol Group. Also to Petty Officer Wayne Stewart of the *Wilson,* whose pictures are here published for the first time; and Harold K. Faye, whose map is based on the chart of the *Mayaguez*. Some of my *Time* colleagues in the Washington Bureau deserve special thanks for providing me with their reports, particularly: Hugh Sidey, Dean E. Fischer, Joseph J. Kane, Strobe Talbott, Jerrold L. Schecter, and Neil MacNeil.

Thanks for rapid and efficient service are due to the entire staff of W. W. Norton & Company and especially to Michelle Cliff, copy editor, and Andrew Marasia, trade production supervisor. Their extraordinary work, together with that of Haddon Craftsmen, the manufacturers, made possible what is surely a modern record of complete clothbound books only four days after delivery of the manuscript.

Roy Rowan

Hong Kong
25 July 1975

A Note on Dates

The four days—Monday through Thursday—of the divisions of this book were, because of the international dateline, Sunday through Wednesday in Washington.

Monday, May 12

ONE

Sattahip-Bound

SHE WAS UNSLEEK. A fresh coat of black covered the rusted pimples and pores of thirty-one years' running and painted out the big starboard dimple where some overzealous tug had shoved her hard against the dock. Through shipyard surgery she had been broadened in the beam, even cut in two and stretched out to carry more cargo, and then welded back together again. And she had borne four names—none of them memorable—*White Falcon, Santa Eliana, Sea,* and *Mayaguez.* Now as she plodded northwest across the Gulf of Thailand at 12.5 knots, a fountain of green foam licked her bow. Flying fish darted out ahead and skimmed the flat sun-drenched sea.

Anastacio Sereno stood behind the wheel gazing out over the sea with his good right eye. He was fifteen minutes more than halfway through his afternoon watch, numbed by the vibration from the old steam turbine coming up through seven decks into the soles of his sneakers. The gyro-pilot was doing the steering. But "Nas," as he was known, glanced down at the compass from time to time to make sure it was still on 318 degrees.

Sereno had boarded the *Mayaguez* in Oakland on October 12. It was only his third ship, not counting the floating cannery he had worked on as a "shaker" up in Alaska. The shaker's job was to shake the meat out of the king crabs onto a conveyor after a butcher had split open the shells. Women canners working further down the conveyor then packed the loose crabmeat into tins. Eleven women lived aboard the ship. They were a lot of trouble, recalled Sereno, and the main reason he quit.

Aboard the *Mayaguez* Sereno was an ordinary seaman. Being a tall, strong man of forty-four and an exceptionally willing worker, he would have been upgraded to able-bodied seaman if it hadn't been for his glass left eye, which barred him from advancement, and which he kept concealed behind steel-rimmed dark glasses day and night.

Sereno stared straight ahead through the three center windows of the wheelhouse, past the steel containers, stacked like giant shoe boxes, two-high and six-abreast, atop the five forward hatches. Beyond the boxes the foremast rose and fell gently against the fluffy cumulus wreath hanging over the horizon. Sporadically, Sereno turned his good eye to scan the horizon. But his thoughts were far away. Just recently he had received a letter from the U.S. Immigration office in San Francisco advising him that he was now eligible to take his examination for American citizenship. He and his three brothers and three sisters were Filipino. But his wife, Roberta, was American. "When I get home in October," he thought, "I'll become an American."

He glanced down at the magnifying glass on the compass. "Three eighteen," he called out to Third Mate Burt Coombes, standing outside the wheelhouse on the starboard wing.

Burton B. Coombes, or "BB" as he was sometimes called, was hardly the picture of an old sea dog—or natty golfer either—even though he good-naturedly referred to himself as the Sam Snead of the S.S. *Mayaguez.* His spikey grey hair was clippered down to the scalp above both ears and on the back of his head. His once-brawny chest had some years earlier slid into the soft sloping beer belly now overhanging his khaki shorts. And his suede Hush Puppies were spattered with white paint drippings. But Burt Coombes's hazel eyes always twinkled, even when he was on watch. Especially when he said things like: "No captain has to tell me 'I don't want you sittin' down on watch,' because I can't sit down very long anyway. You see I got a starboard list." Burt's right leg was slightly shorter than his left, a discovery made back when he was a golf star at Alameda High. First, the doctors tried to stretch it. Then they prescribed a high heel. Neither remedy worked. Now whenever Burt sits down his right hip hurts and he gets fidgety.

When the OS, Sereno, called out: "three eighteen," Burt Coombes looked out at the lush tropical profile of Poulo Wai. The ship's trackline was 323 degrees. But she had been running a little inside, so Burt had changed her course 5 degrees to the left to keep well off the island. "Three eighteen is temporary," he had told Sereno. He guessed the ship was almost back on course now.

Coombes was a seasoned mate. Except for five years ashore with the Wilshire Oil Company in Richmond, California he had gone to sea ever since he got out of high school, though he had never bothered to get his master's ticket. "I always figured if I did, I'd never quit," he would explain.

Partly blocking Burt Coombes's view, from where he stood just outside the wheelhouse door, was the enormous grey arm of the twenty-five–ton crane, folded down into its seagoing position. The two big hydraulic cranes—one fore and one aft—enabled the *Mayaguez* to load and unload herself, a critical capability for a container ship on this Southeast Asia run. Modern port facilities could not always be counted upon. But the powerful cranes could lift and lower the twenty-five–ton containers so fast the *Mayaguez* rarely overnighted anywhere. "She's a here-today-gone-tomorrow ship," complained her crew. Coombes didn't care. At fifty-five he was more interested in a round of golf than a night on the town.

He glanced at his watch: 2:18. Time to take another bearing. Ordinarily, Coombes would use his old Plath sextant, a prized souvenir because it had a German swastika on it, to get his bearing. But with the island in clear view there was no need to do that. He stepped up on the raised platform at the end of the starboard wing, and hunched over the azimuth circle to take a tangent bearing on Poulo Wai. First he lined up the slot and crosshair on the western tip of the island. His eyeglasses were pushed back on top of his head. He didn't need them for distance, only for the chart or compass. In fact, at distances he was "old Eagle-eye," a name his daughter, Linda, had bestowed years ago. She had always marveled at the way he could read the movie marquee from three blocks away. Then he swung the azimuth circle a few degrees to the right to the eastern tip of the island. By sighting both ends of Poulo Wai, Burt could establish the *Mayaguez*'s exact position. As he traversed the middle of the island, a patch of white caught his eye: the bow wave of a fishing boat, he guessed. He finished taking his bearing, then put the binoculars on the boat. White spray was whipping off her bow. A red flag flapped from her mast. Burt Coombes stepped back inside the pilot house and picked the phone off the bulkhead behind Sereno.

"There's a launch with a red flag comin' at us, Captain," he said.

Captain Charles T. Miller had five thousand dollars in stacks of hundreds, fifties, twenties, tens, and fives spread out on his desk when the telephone rang. Charlie Miller hated interruptions in his paper work. "They give me so much paper work I need a goddamn secretary," he had just announced in the officers' saloon, eating his hot pastrami sandwich—one implication being that Mr. Newman, the fat perspiring new chief mate, might volunteer to take a little more of the paper work off his hands. But on any ship it was the master who handled the draw. Captain Miller liked to have the draw ready by suppertime. That way, he figured, I don't have to break anybody out of bed to get their money.

When the phone rang Charlie Miller was bent over his desk cutting up old cargo plans into small strips. On each he wrote the crew member's name and the amount of money he had elected to draw for Sattahip, the port in Thailand where the *Mayaguez* was due to dock at nine o'clock the next morning. Then he counted out the correct amount of cash and clipped the paper to it. Good idea, he decided. Now I won't get confused and go handing out fifties instead of twenties when the man comes to collect. Mistakes like that, he knew, come out of the captain's pocket.

Charlie glanced up at the brass ship's clock above his desk: 2:19. He stood up. A small compact man, a shade under five feet five with wavy salt-and-pepper hair, he had to reach up for the telephone on the pale green bulkhead. Coombes, he had already decided, was probably calling down to tell him the ship wasn't making quite enough speed to reach Sattahip on schedule. This morning Charlie figured they'd be early, so he had cut the steam back to fifteen nozzles.

"There's a launch with a red flag comin' at us," he heard Coombes say.

"I'll be right up," answered Charlie Miller. He swept the stacks of bills off his desk, stepped into his adjoining stateroom and tossed the money into the bottom of his safe. A black mace gun rested atop the safe. Ship captains used to carry revolvers in case a crew member ran amok. Now most skippers carry mace guns instead. It was the only weapon aboard the *Mayaguez*. Charlie left the safe open, but he locked the outer closet door and hurried upstairs.

For a sixty-two-year-old man, just a couple of years away from retirement, he was still pretty spry. He covered the first flight to the bridge two steps at a time, nothing unusual, though, since Charlie was one of those captains who bounded up to the bridge twelve or fifteen times a day, anyway. By now the helmsmen on the *Mayaguez* had gotten used to him popping into the wheelhouse even in the middle of the night. Why not? It was his ship. As Robert E. Fall, the Sea-Land Service, Inc. port captain in San Francisco always told him: "When you let go the lines to the dock, Charlie, she's your ship."

Captain Miller had taken over as master of the *Mayaguez* on January 27, after the *Rose City*, his last ship, had been sold to the

Puerto Rican Navigation and Steamship Company. The *Mayaguez* was smaller, and for Charlie meant a $300-a-month cut in pay. But Sea-Land had promised him a bigger ship as soon as one became available. Anyway, he was planning to start a vacation—three months on the beach—in a little more than six weeks. Ann, his wife, would be flying out to join him in Hong Kong. "I got a good little Polack there," he often bragged. Then he would correct himself. "Actually, she's a Slovak."

He reached the old bridge, now stripped of all its navigational gear, passed the radio shack, and bounded up the last flight of steps into the chartroom. The bridge of the *Mayaguez* had been raised one deck when it had been first converted into a container ship back in 1959. The added height was required to provide an unobstructed view over the deckload of containers.

Sweeping past the chart spread out over the navigation table, Charlie glanced at the trackline marked in heavy pencil. He could see the ship's two o'clock position which Burt Coombes had penciled lightly just inside the trackline. Coombes is a pretty good third, he thought. Always knows where he's at. Better than the last guy, who was always getting lost. Never knew which side of the trackline he was on, which was why Charlie called him Columbus.

"Columbus didn't know where he was goin' either," he used to tell him. "Thought he was going to the East Indies and ended up in the West Indies." Another thing which had made Charlie mad, was his fingernails. "They were three-quarters of an inch long. Like a goddamn Chinaman's," Charlie swore. "He couldn't even pick up the dividers. I finally made him chop them off."

As he popped through the curtain into the wheelhouse, Captain Miller saw his third mate leaning out the open starboard window, his head hunched forward against his binoculars. Guided by the direction Coombes was looking, he picked up the onrushing boat at first glance. It was still a mile away: a grey sliver churning the glassy turquoise expanse separating the *Mayaguez* from Poulo Wai. Charlie grabbed his own binoculars, prefocused and ready for him to pick up. None of the mates would dare touch them.

The grey sliver, he saw instantly, was a gunboat. Magnified, he could see the gunboat throwing spray off her bow, doing eighteen or twenty knots, coming straight at the *Mayaguez* at a ninety-degree angle. He could just make out the machine gun atop the pilot house. Still peering through his binoculars, he heard the first burst of fifteen or twenty rounds of machine-gun fire. They must be using tracers, he realized. He could see the trail of white smoke across his bow.

"Give me maneuvering speed!" he shouted.

Burt Coombes was standing by the engine room telephone anticipating the command. He jerked the phone off the bulkhead. "Maneuvering speed!" he barked. "Give me maneuvering speed!"

Burt Coombes had been under fire before—twice actually, counting the torpedo he once spotted coming towards the *H.T. Harper*, a Standard Oil tanker. But it was aboard the Liberty ship *John Burgess,* on which he had seen real action. The *Burgess* had been in the first convoy to enter Lingayen Gulf after General MacArthur's landing. On many ships since then Coombes had recounted the ill-fated voyage. "Our own battleships were shooting over our heads into the hills, and Jap Zeros were dive-bombing us at the same time," he would explain. "The ship managed to get out of there okay. But the crew wasn't so lucky. Some of the guys had got into the wood alcohol. Two went blind and five died."

Burt had barely hung up the phone, when he heard the gunboat fire a second burst. The noise was louder this time.

"Put her on hand telemotor," Captain Miller snapped. Coombes watched Sereno shove the gyro-pilot lever forward to off, and push down the telemotor transfer switch in back of the wheel. The *Mayaguez* was now being steered by hand.

Captain Miller, a little rooster of a man in white shirt and khaki pants, stood framed in the wheelhouse door, watching the gunboat keep to its collision course. Burt could see the captain's jaw jut and his nostrils flare. He was mad. The machine gun erupted again.

Suddenly Coombes caught the blur of a dark object hurtling over their bow.

"Captain, there goes a goddamn rocket," he said. The explosion sent a geyser of water into the air.

TWO

The Black Gang's Messenger

FIRST ENGINEER VERN GREENLIN crossed the high catwalk heading for the electrical shop when he heard the telephone down on the operating platform, forty feet below, bray like a burglar alarm. On the *Mayaguez* the engineroom telephone buzzer had to be loud and insistent enough to penetrate the deafening clank and whine of the ship's ancient power plant. Other parts of the ship had been enlarged and modernized. The engineroom, though, remained in its original state, virtually unaltered since the ship passed its first sea trials on April 24, 1944. A forest of grimy silver pipes grew up around the catwalk like oozing stalagmites. Oil-stained plywood boards covered the catwalk's iron grating to keep dirt from dropping down and fouling the machinery below. There was nothing unusual about a telephone call from the bridge, so Greenlin, with the sweat seeping through his navy blue coveralls, continued on his way to the electrical shop located just outside the engineroom on the starboard side of the shelter deck. Anyway, he could imagine what the call was about. Probably was the captain. The old man was always asking for maneuvering speed: 12 nozzles and 60 rpm, to get through a fleet of fishing boats.

Vernon P. Greenlin's thirty-six years of engineroom experience covered enough ships so he had difficulty remembering half of them. The Greenlins were a seafaring family. His father had worked on ships, until he decided to stay on the beach in San

Francisco and drive a streetcar. But after so many years at sea, Greenlin's real interest was now prospecting for gold. He had staked out two claims in the High Sierras. Gold mining was what he wanted to get into when he retired, even though Jeanne, his wife, didn't care for the Sierras. She preferred to stay at home in Santa Rosa.

The round trip to the electrical shop took Greenlin approximately sixty seconds. As he retraced his steps across the catwalk he heard the bell to stop engines. He glanced at his watch: 2:21. Peering down through the maze of pipes and four levels of catwalks, he could see Third Engineer Al Minichiello begin to turn the green wheel of the "ahead" throttle to the right, closing off the steam to the high pressure turbine. Greenlin grabbed the hot handrails and half-slid down the first ladder. As first engineer he didn't stand a watch. His job was primarily to keep the old engineroom machinery from breaking down. But a stop-engines bell out in the middle of the Gulf of Thailand was unexpected. He wanted to find out what in hell was going on.

Oiler Americo Faria stepped out on the cabin deck and sucked in the fresh sea air. As always when he was on watch, he had a sweat-drenched handkerchief knotted around his white hair. Even so, dribbles of perspiration rolled down his temples and caught in little pools in the hollows under his eyes. A large beefy man, 225 pounds and a shade under six feet, Faria had a white, almost embalmed look about him, as if the steamy sunless hours down in the engineroom had boiled all the pigment out of his skin.

But Faria hadn't come up from the engineroom to cool off. Once a watch he had to go back to the stern and oil the steering engine. On the *Mayaguez* there was no way to get to the steering engine without going outside, so he had paused for a moment to light his pipe and look out at the lush tropical island off the starboard bow. He had passed that island many times before, aboard the *Trans-Colorado.* But Faria had never seen the island so close up. Now he could make out the strip of white sand beach six or seven miles away. He wished he was over on that beach having a swim. As a boy in New Bedford, Massachusetts he had grown up taking cooling ocean dips on the hot summer afternoons. Suddenly, a grey boat caught his eye—coming straight for the *Mayaguez.* A refugee boat, he figured. "So now we're going to be picking up refugees," he said to himself. Then he heard the first burst of machine-gun fire. Flabbergasted, Faria stood watching the boat still speeding straight at them. There was a second burst and Faria beat it over to the port side to get out of the line of fire.

On the boat deck directly above Oiler Faria, Ordinary Seaman Gerardo Lopez, a Mexican-American with a wide laughing face, was painting the davit of lifeboat No. 1. It wasn't Lopez's watch, but he was glad to be working overtime and earning extra money. He had two children in high school back in New Orleans.

As he sighted along the *Mayaguez's* rippled and bent railings and surveyed the cratered deck plates, Lopez said to himself: "We could spend all our days chipping and painting this old ship, but she'd still look sad." In Hong Kong, four days earlier, the black hull had been repainted by a shore crew. And on the trip before that, the ship had gone into dry dock in Hong Kong and gotten her bottom scaled and recoated with anti-fouling compound. But no amount of paint seemed to brighten the *Mayaguez.* She was a work ship. And as if to emphasize the *Mayaguez's* working status, a hodge-podge of wire cables, drums of chemicals, bags of sawdust, paint, hawsers, ladders, droplights, and assorted shipboard impedimenta lay strewn around her decks. Only the bridge and boat deck were kept reasonably tidy. Between them, OS Gerardo Lopez with a paint brush, and AB Earl Gilbert with a hurdy-gurdy, as the compressed-air chipping hammers are called, were tidying up the starboard side of the boat deck a little more.

Gilbert's hurdy-gurdy chattering away against the davit on the other end of the lifeboat, was making such a racket that Lopez didn't even hear the first machine-gun burst. He kept right on painting.

"Lopez, get off the deck!" he heard AB Tom LaBue shout from above. "The captain says get off the deck!"

Lopez saw Earl Gilbert throw down the hurdy-gurdy and duck inside. Before he could put away his paint brush the second machine-gun burst ripped the air. They don't have to tell me to get off the deck, he thought. Lopez dropped the brush and ran inside. Out the open door on the port side, he could see his friend, Polo Vasquez, still chipping away on lifeboat No. 2.

"Come inside, Polo!" Lopez shouted in Spanish. "Polo, come inside. They are shooting at us."

"Who's shooting at us?" laughed Polo Vasquez.

"Polo, I don't know. There's a boat shooting at us."

"Bullshit!" said Polo in English.

"No bullshit, Polo. It's true. Hurry up. Come inside." Lopez watched Americo Faria, his undershirt plastered with sweat against his big white stomach, come huffing up the ladder to the boat deck.

"We're being captured," shouted Faria to Polo Vasquez. But Polo was now surer than ever that he was being bullshitted. He put down his hurdy-gurdy and stood smiling at the big perspiring oiler. At that moment the rocket exploded and he and Faria dove in through the open doorway. "We've been hit," yelled Faria, who had failed to see the geyser of water erupt off the port bow. "They hit the boxes up forward. Must be a hell of a hole up there."

Lopez could visualize the hole, all right. On his first ship, the *Steel Traveller,* they had been hit by two rockets. The attack came while the ship was still tied up at the dock. It was in some Cambodian port. Lopez couldn't remember the name. But he remembered the date: January 27, 1973, the day they signed the Peace Accords in Paris. It took eight days to weld a temporary patch to the side of the *Steel Traveller* so they could leave. "We are lucky,"

Lopez had written home to his wife, Luvia. "Nobody is hurt. But there are two big holes in our ship."

Vern Greenlin didn't fluster easily. A handsome, black-haired man, described by one of his firemen as "handsomer than Boris Karloff," he kept his feelings pretty much to himself. In the officers' saloon he usually ate in silence rather than enter into the daily banter or bickering, neither of which he cared for. Greenlin tended to agree with that old shipboard saying: "Sailors are like seagulls. All they do is eat, squawk, and shit."

But as he shot down the last ladder from the high catwalk to the operating platform at the bottom of the engineroom, Greenlin felt a twinge of excitement running through him. Third Engineer Al Minichiello, he saw, had already finished closing the ahead throttle, had opened the guardian valve and was just commencing to open the red astern throttle, to brake the high pressure turbine. Minichiello was new. He had just joined the *Mayaguez* in Hong Kong. He had to hold onto his right wrist with his left hand when he signed the engineroom log at the end of his watch. For that reason Greenlin wanted to make doubly sure Minichiello had everything under control.

Greenlin's shoes hit the rippled steel floor plates with a whack. He glanced back up the ladder and saw Faria, the heavy white-haired oiler with the handkerchief knotted around his head, coming down practically on top of him. He was moving fast, the sweat flying off his hulking white shoulders. "Jesus Christ," said Faria, landing next to Greenlin. "We're being captured."

"Captured?" said the first engineer. "By who?"

"How the hell do I know?" said Faria. "All I know is there was a hell of an explosion up on the bow. Somebody's shootin' at the forward boxes."

Twice before Greenlin had had ships sunk out from under him. He had been torpedoed aboard the Liberty ship *John Adams* off Noumea. The *Adams* was carrying gas in drums and she went up like a torch. Greenlin always remembered how the Jap sub had surfaced and shined its light on the two lifeboats, then let them row away. The only men killed were the eight Navy gunners who jumped overboard before the lifeboats could be launched. Another time, aboard the *Andrea Luckenbach,* the captain had been trying to sneak too close to Kauai Island in Hawaii and ran aground. Tore a big hole in the bottom and they never did get the ship off. She was a C-2 just like the *Mayaguez,* he recalled.

For an instant Greenlin was tempted to run up topside and see for himself who was shooting at them. Then he decided not to. If we're really sinking, he thought, we'll know soon enough. Hell, it could be pirates. Just that morning he and the chief had been talking about how there were still pirates holding up ships in the South China Sea.

Over on the other side of the turbine, he could see Faria telling fireman Guerrero the news.

Carlos Guerrero had just finished changing burners and was back at his regular station, standing under the big blower in front of the boilers, when Faria came over and started yelling something into his ear. The clank of the bull-gear and the two banks of roaring oil-fed fires made it almost impossible to hear anything. Besides, Guerrero, who came from Honduras, didn't understand Faria's English too well, even though they were cabin-mates.

"Hey, Guerrero, we're being captured," is what he thought Faria was shouting into his ear.

Guerrero nodded his head and smiled. Faria was making a joke.

"No bullshit, Guerrero, we're being captured," repeated Faria.

Guerrero nodded and smiled again. Then he tilted his head up so the tip of his tan baseball cap almost touched the rim of the blower. He remained in that position letting the rush of cool air freeze the sweat on his face. Faria, he thought, he's always trying to fool me. Guerrero's eyes followed the old white-haired oiler now walking towards the machine shop to try his joke on the new wiper.

Wiper Tyrone J. Matthews—"Poppy" his mother called him—
had been broke and on the beach in Yokohama before he joined
the *Mayaguez* three weeks ago. Black, thirty-five, and married and
separated twice, Matthews felt a powerful attraction for Asia—
even for Vietnam, where as a Special Forces sergeant he had made
eighteen practice parachute jumps getting ready for the real thing.
But they shipped him back home and off to the Dominican Republic before he could jump in combat. "Vietnam was a hell of an
experience," he often told his shipmates, who thought he was
crazy. "I loved the culture, the violence, the corruption. It was all
beautiful."

On many ships over the past ten years, Matthews had worked
on deck and in the galley, as well as with the Black Gang in the
engineroom. But he liked the Black Gang best. "You can learn
things down in the engineroom," he said. This, of course, was true,
especially on the *Mayaguez,* where the machinery was always
breaking down. But Matthews liked the *Mayaguez* for other rea-
sons. "Man, on this ship," he often said, "the engineers are beautiful."

Matthews had just come out of the machine shop, which is
enclosed behind a white wire-mesh bulkhead on the port side of the
engineroom, when he ran into Faria.

"Hey, Matthews," said Faria. "We're being captured!"

"Captured?" said the wiper smiling. "That's beautiful."

"No bullshit. We're being captured. They're shooting at us. Hit
the boxes up forward with a big rocket."

Suddenly Matthews wasn't sure it was beautiful. Seven years
ago going up the Saigon River on the *Trans-Globe,* the Viet Cong
had hit the ship with an armor-piercing shell and killed his good
Hawaiian buddy, Ernie Gu. They blew Ernie up in his room while
he was brushing his teeth, Matthews remembered.

"Who's shooting at us?" he asked.

"How the hell do I know," said Faria. "I come straight down
here. Go ask the chief. Maybe he knows."

Vern Greenlin was standing in front of the little half-enclosed telephone booth next to the throttles, figuring he might get a call from the bridge with some new information, when the earsplitting buzzer went off. He grabbed the phone. It was Coombes. "We're being fired on by a Cambodian gunboat," said the third mate. Then Coombes hung up.

Before they sailed from Hong Kong, Greenlin had read a newspaper account of the growing border dispute between Cambodia and Thailand. The story described unprovoked attacks on unarmed Thai fishing boats by Cambodian gunboats. But hell, he thought, we ain't no fishing boat.

Anyway, he didn't have the chance to reflect on their situation further. Cliff Harrington, the chief engineer, had just emerged from the diesel room and seemed to be looking for him. Harrington was a pretty decent guy, Greenlin thought. Capable chief and easygoing. Never hard-assed you as long as you did your job. Actually, Greenlin generally sailed as chief himself. His last job had been chief engineer aboard the *Fairland.* But during the summer his doctor had discovered a small throat cancer, necessitating a series of laser beam treatments. They kept Greenlin on the beach. But with Harrington, he didn't really mind being first assistant.

"Where you been, Chief?" he asked as Harrington came down off the ladder. "We've been captured by Cambodians."

"Cambodians? We aren't even at war with Cambodia." Harrington's voice cracked with surprise, the way Jimmy Stewart's voice used to crack in the movies. Lanky, with slicked-back reddish hair, Harrington in fact looked a great deal like Jimmy Stewart. People were always coming up to him and asking: "Say, did anyone ever tell you you look like Jimmy Stewart?"

Suddenly Harrington realized why it was so quiet in the engine-room. The high pressure turbine was shut down. When he had first stepped out of the diesel room it sounded awful quiet. But he decided it was his ears, that he had been temporarily deafened by the wild banshee screech of the diesel-driven generators. He had been cooped up with the infernal machines for half an hour trying to install a new exhaust pipe on the turbo-charger. The exhaust pipe was secured by a flange which had already broken off several times. The hell with it, Harrington had finally decided, I'm going to make the bolts heavier. So he had drilled new holes and was just going down to pick up a tap and get the first engineer to help him tap them in, when he ran into Greenlin.

"Vern, you're not shitting me," he said. Harrington had been going to sea on and off for thirty-seven years, ever since he'd first escorted a bunch of Army mules to Manila on an old Hog Islander named the *Meigs*. But in his whole career he had never heard of a merchant ship being captured.

"How do you know we've been captured?" he asked.

"Faria just came down. He was up on deck. Saw the gunboat fire a rocket into the forward boxes."

Harrington's first instinct was to grab the telephone and call the old man. No, he thought, I'll wait for him to call me. He's probably got his hands full.

Harrington looked up through the seven levels of ladders and catwalks intertwined with the tangle of multi-colored pipes—silver for steam, yellow for lube oil, black for fuel oil, green for water, but smeared so dark with oil you could hardly tell the colors apart —and wondered, what in Christ's name am I doing on a rust-pot like this? Most chiefs won't even take one of these beat-up old C-2s. And now we're being captured.

Then it hit him. Suppose the Cambodians come down here shooting. They're going to pick us off like sitting ducks. Years ago he had seen an old Charlie Chan movie where a band of Chinese pirates dropped hand grenades down into the engineroom. The entire Black Gang was either riddled by shrapnel or scalded to death by steam from the exploding boilers and pipes. And in real life, during the invasion of Eniwetok, he had sat out on the deck of the *Cape Trinity* and watched a bunch of Japs get chased out into the water and shot to pieces. The next day, he remembered, he had gone ashore and looked at the Japs all bloated and black from the sun, lying on the beach. He wondered if the crew of the *Mayaguez* would look like that when the Cambodians got finished with them.

Well, there's one thing we can do, he thought. We can pull the master switch and turn out all the lights in the engineroom. We, at least, know our way around in the dark. The Cambodians would have a hell of a time finding us. The thought of turning out the lights began to grow on Harrington. He told Greenlin. "Maybe they'd kill us in the end," he said. "But goddamnit, they'd have to find us first."

Harrington walked back to the shaft alley. The steam was shut down on the turbine, but he could tell the ship was still coasting forward. The force of the water was turning the big 19-foot propeller and rotating the 150-foot-long grey shaft. Harrington could visualize his engineroom crew cowering at the far end of the shaft alley as the Cambodians took aim and used it for a shooting gallery.

Might as well make it tough on them, he thought. Then he reached up and commenced to turn the red handle that lowered the watertight door at the entrance to the shaft alley. He kept turning the handle until the inch-thick steel door was almost closed. Only an eighteen-inch opening remained at the bottom. He called to Greenlin to come over.

"Okay, Vern," he said. "If the Cambodians come down shooting, I'll pull the master switch and we'll all crawl back into the shaft alley on our bellies."

The first engineer nodded. "Tell the Black Gang," said Harrington.

THREE

The Seizure

CAPTAIN CHARLES MILLER eyed his interceptor skipping towards him over the turquoise sea, with more indignation than fear. He had to stop the ship. Shots across the bow meant one thing: stop or be sunk, and a rocket like the one which had just exploded in the water could rip a big hole in the *Mayaguez*. But the little gunboat's audacity made him boil. If I had the speed, he thought, I'd show the sonofabitch our tail and let him catch us.

At sixty-two, there was still plenty of feistiness in Charlie Miller. It gleamed out of his blue eyes, and was further attested to by the small white scars variously situated around his face. "When I was a mate," he liked to tell the mates on the *Mayaguez*, "and I caught a sailor lounging in a deck chair on my watch, I used to beat the shit out of him." Charlie made it known he didn't only pick on underlings. Once he served under a tough old Dalmatian skipper who was something of a legend around American President Lines for cussing out and then firing almost every mate who ever worked for him. The skipper called Charlie a sonofabitch. "I hit him on the back of the head with the China Coast Pilot book," Charlie said. "He looked surprised. But he never called me a sonofabitch again, and I made four more trips with him."

Already Charlie could feel the pulse in the deck under his feet start to fade. From the *Mayaguez* bridge, the 6,000-horsepower GE engine was never very loud. But you could always feel it in your feet. Charlie listened, anyway. He worried that the *Mayaguez* might not be slowing down fast enough to keep the gunboat from throwing another rocket over his bow. All he could hear was the hum of the reefers on the foredeck and the faint hiss of the hull coasting through the water.

"Did Sparks get out the SOS?" he snapped at Burt Coombes.

Coombes had just come back on the bridge. He had started to go downstairs to the radio shack with a slip of paper marked: 09–48N 102–53E, the ship's position at 2:18 off Poulo Wai, when he met Sparks coming up. As he thrust the piece of paper into Wilbert Bock's hand, he could feel it trembling. Funny, Coombes thought, I don't feel scared. But he suddenly remembered that on previous ships he had always carried a sealed letter addressed to the captain in his pocket. "In the event of my death, please bury me at sea," the letter instructed. For some reason he hadn't bothered to bring it on the *Mayaguez.*

"I gave Sparks our position, Captain," Coombes answered.

"But did he get the SOS out?" Captain Miller snapped again.

"Sparks said he already got it out with our noon position, Captain. Two or three times. Said an English ship and a Norwegian ship had received it."

Charlie Miller gave no indication that he had heard his third mate. His gaze and attention were homed in on the gunboat, suddenly close enough to read the 128 painted in white numerals on its bow. The gunboat made a taunting sweep in front of the *Mayaguez.* As it turned, sun caught the belted ammo which was hanging down from the twin-fifty-calibre machine gun mounted atop the pilot house. For an instant the reflected light came back to the bridge of the *Mayaguez* in rapid-fire flashes, just like the gun was shooting. There was a second, single-barrel anti-aircraft gun and a rocket-launcher mounted on the after deck. Though manned, their barrels all pointed skyward. For an instant, as the gunboat completed its sweep and came up on a course parallel with the *Mayaguez,* Charlie Miller wondered whether the crazy gooks,

Cambodians or whoever they were, were going to lower their barrels and start blazing away.

David Christopher English, twenty-eight years old and a 250-pound ex-Marine with wild carrot-colored hair and a moustache to match, had given up trying to sleep. On the other side of the half-inch–thick steel bulkhead, right next to where his head was resting on the pillow, the deck gang was chipping away with their hurdy-gurdies. They might just as well have been pounding his head with sledgehammers.

As the eight-to-twelve third mate, English was in the habit of taking a nap after lunch. As usual he had taken his shoes and socks off. Otherwise he was fully dressed. Fat freckled legs stuck out of his khaki shorts. A hefty stomach ballooned out the front of his white T-shirt. Three years ago in Seattle, English had been stricken with pancreatitis. His weight had shot up from 186 to 290, and while it had now receded, there was still a heavy layer of fat concealing his powerful muscles. Miraculously, as if the deck gang had somehow heard his obscene thoughts, the chipping hammers suddenly stopped exploding in his ear. Dave English glanced at his watch: 2:21. No use trying to sleep now, he thought. Not with a fire and boat drill at 3:15. He picked up his *Time* magazine and started to read.

The peace and quiet didn't last very long. In the companionway outside his cabin, he could hear the steward and a bunch of sailors jabbering away. English threw open the door. "What the hell's going on?" he bellowed. You could always hear one of English's bellows a couple of decks away.

"There's a gunboat shootin' at us," said the steward. English could tell Erv Anderson was excited. But he didn't believe him. "Come on Anderson," he said.

"I wouldn't lie to you about a thing like that," said Anderson, his face gleaming with sweat.

English put on his shoes and socks and hurried outside. The gunboat was just swinging around the bow of the *Mayaguez*. He recognized it instantly. It was a swiftboat: an American-built craft, the kind they used in Vietnam to protect the fishing fleets. In August 1964, English had been a Marine onboard the U.S.S. *Benville* out in the Gulf of Tonkin, when the North Vietnamese PT boats attacked. He and the rest of the Marines sat out on deck watching the American destroyers shoot back at the PTs. "When the first PT sank everybody applauded," he had written home to his father, who had commanded an American gunboat in Panama during World War II. After that his Marine unit had sat out in the Gulf of Tonkin for almost three months. "We all sent our absentee ballots in for Johnson," he had also written home. "We figure if Goldwater is elected we'll have to go ashore and fight." English ended up going ashore and fighting in Vietnam anyway.

English watched the gunboat pull up on a course parallel to the *Mayaguez*. A red flag as big as a bed sheet was flapping from its mast. He could see the twin-fifty mounted on the wheelhouse with a little fellow swinging around behind it. That guy could hit us with no trouble at all, he thought. But why the hell are we stopping? We're sixty miles off the coast.

Chief Mate James Patrick Newman joined the *Mayaguez* in Hong Kong on May 7, the day before she sailed for Sattahip. A roly-poly, friendly man, he was sitting in his little office next to the officers' saloon when AB Earl Gilbert burst in and blurted: "Hey, Chief, somebody's shootin' at us!"

"Shootin' at us? What do you mean, Gilbert?"

For thirty-one years, since he first set out from New York harbor on an old Hog Islander, the *Alcoa Cutter*, Newman had sailed the world's oceans without ever coming under fire. At least not gunfire. Most of his captains—and Charlie Miller was no exception—were forever shooting him down, mainly because his tubbiness and gentle good nature made him such an easy target.

"There's a boat out there shootin' at us," Gilbert explained. Newman raised his heavy body out of his swivel chair. Once he had encountered enemy action of a sort. On the *Maiden Creek,* up in the North Sea, they had hit an old acoustic mine. Blew hell out of the engineroom, he remembered.

"You serious?" Newman said.

"Go out and take a look for yourself, Chief," urged Gilbert. Instead of going out, Newman hurried as fast as he could up the three flights of stairs to the wheelhouse. Nobody was shooting at them. But a mast with an oversize red flag flapping from it was running alongside, barely twenty feet from the *Mayaguez.*

"Newman," barked the captain when he saw his new chief mate come puffing into the wheelhouse, "get a deck gang down there and put a ladder over the side."

The chief mate went back downstairs, Sereno following after him. AB Tom LaBue had taken over the helm, and Sereno figured he'd better go down and give the chief mate a hand.

"What's going on?" asked Newman.

"Don't know," said Sereno. "He just came out from behind that island and started shooting at us." Mr. Newman wasn't worried. But for the first time since he had gone to sea, he envied his brother Eugene, a toll plaza supervisor on the New Jersey Turnpike. Now Gene, he thought, he's got the right kind of job. You can't get into trouble like this out on the Jersey Turnpike.

Sereno followed the chief mate down to the main deck. The *Mayaguez* was still coasting forward at about a quarter-speed. A 10,485-ton ship with 274 containers on it, he knew, doesn't stop easily. Not even with the kick of its propeller gone. Gradually though, she was losing momentum. Her sponsons, the empty steel chambers which had been grafted onto her formerly skinny hull like a pair of false bosoms—to provide the beam and buoyancy necessary for the big containers—also acted as a brake. Sereno could hear the sea gurgling against the sponsons as he and Mr. Newman came out on deck.

The two men hurried forward along the narrow pathway between the containers and the starboard rail. The gunboat had
already come alongside. Less than twenty feet of water separated
the two ships, the scaly black hull of the *Mayaguez* now looming
over the sleek grey gunboat which was holding her at bay.

There were a lot of things Sereno simply didn't understand: like
why the manager of the Roadway Inn in San Francisco had let him
go just because he couldn't drive a car. After all, he had been a very
good bellman. Or, for that matter, how he happened to end up on
the *Mayaguez.* He'd been sitting around the SIU hall at Ninth and
Mission for eighty-nine days with no luck. On the ninetieth day his
shipping card would have expired. But a call had come in for an
ordinary seaman on the *Mayaguez,* and they picked him to fill the
job. Now there was another thing he didn't understand. How could
a little gunboat stop a big ship like the *Mayaguez* far out at sea.

The top of the gunboat was even with the main deck of the
Mayaguez. Sereno glanced over, and his good eye caught the gaze
of a teen-aged boy gripping the handles of the twin-fifty-calibre
machine gun. He can't be more than fourteen or fifteen, Sereno
guessed. But his face was stern. He was holding onto the handles
of the weapon like his life depended on it. Two belts of shiny brass
shells hung down from the double-barreled anti-aircraft gun. It is
fortunate, Sereno thought, that the gun is pointing at the sun,
because the young boy looks nervous, as if it would soothe his
nerves to shoot at something.

"Lower the pilot ladder," Sereno heard Mr. Newman say. He
had already lashed the rope ladder to the railing. Now he let it go
and the wooden rungs slapped against the steel sponsons like they
were beating on a drum.

Sereno watched the gunboat slide closer until its port gunwhale
gave the side of the *Mayaguez* a couple of good cracks. Without
warning a boy in black pajamas leaped onto the ladder and clam-
bered up the side of the *Mayaguez.* He had a rifle over his shoulder.
As he climbed, the gun butt banged against the ship. Then a second

boy caught the ladder and started climbing. They were dressed alike: black pajamas, headbands, and sandals. The third boy was lugging some kind of a heavy rocket-launcher. The weapon was cumbersome and he couldn't make it all the way up the ladder. Sereno, the courteous ex-bellhop from the Roadway Inn in San Francisco, went over the side and lugged the heavy weapon up for him.

"Now why did I do that?" Sereno asked himself as four more Cambodians climbed from the gunboat onto the *Mayaguez.* "I should have let him drop it in the water."

Captain Charles Miller watched the seven black-clad figures scramble up the pilot's ladder and alight on the deck of his ship, with a strange sense of detachment. Perhaps it was his high perch on the starboard wing of the bridge from where he viewed the bizarre scene unfolding below. Or maybe it was the miniature size of the men, or their funny black pajamas which made them appear childlike—toting toy guns and not to be taken seriously. In any case, fear was not one of the emotions surging through the captain as he watched his ship being seized. But he was damn mad, and he was curious. "Well," he said to himself, "we'll find out soon enough what these bastards want." He stepped back into the wheelhouse to wait.

The first man to come through the wheelhouse door was slightly taller than Charlie: five feet six or five feet seven, he guessed, and about 150 pounds. He was older than the others: thirty-three or thirty-four maybe. Slung over his shoulder he had an AK-47 with a scrap of red cloth stuffed into the muzzle to keep dirt or water from getting inside the barrel. In his hand he carried a U.S. Army fieldpack radio. Three men followed him into the wheelhouse, all identically dressed in black pajamas.

"Speak English?" Charlie asked. The man shook his head.

"Parlez-vous Français?" inquired Charlie. He didn't speak French himself, but he had a Cajun pantryman on board by the name of Pastrano—boxer Willie Pastrano's father—whom he knew could speak some French. Again the man shook his head. He just kept looking around the wheelhouse, inspecting the radar, telemotor, gyro-pilot, and the other standard pieces of navigation equipment. Finally the man pointed to the chartroom and motioned for Charlie to go in.

"Cambodge. Baie de Ream," he said glancing at the chart. It was obvious the man had no trouble deciphering the American navigation symbols. Immediately, he put his finger on Poulo Wai, the tropical island that the *Mayaguez* was now abeam of, and which appeared as a pair of fish-shaped atolls on the chart. Then he picked up a pencil and drew a small anchor behind the inner atoll, indicating that's where he wanted the *Mayaguez* to go. "Fathoms or meters?" he asked, suddenly revealing that he knew at least a smattering of English.

"Meters," snapped the captain, though the depths on the chart were given in fathoms. If he thinks the chart's in meters, we'll have an excuse for staying farther offshore, Charlie reasoned. When they returned to the wheelhouse the gunboat was already moving in towards the island. The Cambodian pointed at the gunboat. He wanted Charlie to follow.

"Keep her pointed at the stern of that gunboat," Charlie instructed the AB, Tom LaBue, who was now at the wheel. Then Charlie instinctively reached for the engineroom telephone to ask for twelve nozzles. The Cambodian waggled the barrel of his gun and shook his head. "No," he said using English again. He must think it's a radio, Charlie decided, and he pushed the arm of the ship's telegraph forward to half-ahead. A few moments later he could feel the faint vibration coming up through the deck. No matter what, he wanted to keep the *Mayaguez* moving as slowly as possible.

Once they got underway, Charlie could see his captors begin to relax. The ensign, or whatever the man was who had drawn the anchor on the chart, stepped out on the starboard wing and began

conversing in Cambodian over his fieldpack radio. One boy, beady-
eyed and with his AK-47 laying across his lap, had taken a seat
behind the radar. The two other Cambodians had positioned themselves next to LaBue, to watch him steer the ship. Charlie eased
himself back into the chartroom and out of sight of the Cambodians. Then he hurried below to his cabin. Two pieces of unfinished
business were preying on his mind.

His office and stateroom were exactly as he had left them half
an hour ago. The stack of red-bordered RCA radiograms rested
untouched on the corner of his desk. The neat three-pillow pyra-
mid, which the bedroom steward, Darryl Kastl, always arranged
so perfectly on top of his blue bedspread, was undisturbed. Quickly
Charlie unlocked the closet concealing his safe. The weighted steel
door inside was still open, and the $5,000 in loose bills which he
had been counting out for the draw when Burt Coombes called, lay
scattered over the bottom of the safe. There was another $5,000
wrapped in rubber bands, and an envelope, which as noted on the
outside, contained exactly $11,953. Charlie always knew precisely
how much money he had in the safe. As captain, he was personally
accountable for every penny of it. But more than that, all his life,
it seemed, money had been a problem. Inevitably, he had trouble
holding on to it.

Once during World War II, when he was married to his first
wife, Millicent, Charlie came back from a six-month trip on an
ammunition ship, the *William W. Mayo,* with eight crisp one-
thousand-dollar bills in his pocket. Millicent was all smiles, even
though she had warned Charlie, if he ever went to sea again, not
to come back. The day after he returned, the water heater blew up.
Charlie was down in the basement trying to fix it when a guy drove
up to the house on a three-wheeled motorcycle and handed him a
summons. Millicent, it turned out, had already filed for divorce.
Charlie left the eight one-thousand-dollar bills on the kitchen table
and walked out of the house.

Another time, after he had remarried and quit going to sea,

Charlie became chairman of the board of Western Shipping Corporation, a small company which he had founded himself. Western Shipping's assets consisted of one leased Japanese freighter named the *Kowan Maru*, which earned a marginal profit, and an expensive dream which Charlie had been nurturing for a long time, to establish a World Trade Exhibit ship that would ply the oceans of the world displaying new products. Charlie had already sunk $70,000 of his own money into his dream and his company faced bankruptcy. As a last resort he wrote to President Kennedy. "You may not remember me," Charlie started off. Then he proceeded to explain how during the war down in New Guinea Kennedy had brought his PT 109 alongside a ship named the *Sea Marlin* on which Charlie was third mate. "We had our own ice-cream maker on board," Charlie reminded the president, "and we really fixed you guys up." Kennedy wrote back suggesting that Charlie go see a Mr. Snyder in the Small Business Administration office in Los Angeles. Two days later Kennedy was assassinated and Charlie shipped out for Cam Ranh Bay as third mate aboard the *Vanderbilt Victory*. He was broke.

Charlie stared at the cash piled in the safe. The notion that his captors might force him to open the safe and then make off with all his money, had been worrying him ever since the Cambodians came aboard. There were two built-in wooden drawers under Charlie's bunk. Quickly he removed the left drawer and stuffed the envelope with the $11,953 and all the loose bills into the empty space underneath. Then he replaced the drawer. But the $5,000 wrapped in rubber bands, he left sitting in the safe. It would look suspicious, he thought, if the safe were empty.

Next he grabbed the *Mayaguez*'s Alfa Envelope (No. 104) the secret code and instructions which every U.S. merchant ship carries. Ordinarily, Alfa Envelopes are only to be opened upon radioed instructions from Washington. Charlie ripped open the envelope. He threw the code sheets into his metal wastebasket, squirted lighter fluid on top of them, and tossed in a lighted match.

While the code sheets blazed, he glanced around the room. The naked Chinese girl on his Dairy Lane wall calendar, standing demurely with her two hands covering her private parts, appeared to be winking at him. Finally, he picked up the wastebasket with the charred Alfa Envelope, walked out on deck, and heaved the whole thing, wastebasket and all, into the sea.

By the time Third Mate Dave English, his red hair flying and his temper flaring, reached the bridge Captain Miller was back up in the wheelhouse. They'll be watching the old man like a hawk, English knew. "Maybe I can move around and do a few things for him," he told himself. Big and belligerent, English had already determined not to take any shit from the Cambodians.

The first thing English saw was one of the Cambodians jabbering at the old man and pointing to the gunboat, trying to get him to follow.

"Too shallow, not enough water," Captain Miller kept repeating. He watched the old man go in and point to the chart. "See," he said, "meters, not fathoms. Too shallow."

For a second English thought the old man had slipped his track. The chart was in fathoms. Foxy old bastard, he finally realized. He's trying to keep us away from that island.

Out on the starboard wing, English could see another one of the Cambodians using a walkie-talkie—calling the gunboat, he guessed, or maybe talking to the beach. Suddenly, he remembered Sparks. Jesus, Sparks could be kind of a "juicer." He wondered if Sparks had broadcast their situation—not just the normal SOS on 500 kilocycles, saying they were in distress and giving their position, but a full account of what was going on. It wasn't that he didn't trust Sparks. But by his own admission, English had a negative nature, and he really didn't have much faith in anything. "I always think of the worst thing that can happen," he often said. "Then if something better happens, I've got something to smile about." Some bad things had happened to English. In "Happy

Valley"—"You know, the other side of the mountain from Danang"—he had been shot one time through the left elbow and another time through the left knee. But then some of his best buddies, like Jimmy Dollins from Nantucket, had fared worse. They were killed. On board a tanker, the *Atlantic Engineer,* heading back from Drift River, Alaska with a full load of crude, a fire had broken out and the forward deckhouse opened up like a can of sardines. English luckily had come off watch to eat breakfast. The mate on watch broke his back, the chief mate broke his arm, and the bosun got burned so bad they had to make English bosun.

No, it wasn't that he didn't like Sparks. He's a pretty good guy English thought. But suppose he's not getting the word out.

English backed out of the wheelhouse as unobtrusively as he could, then beat it down to the radio shack. There's no lock on the radio shack door, so English barged in.

"Be quiet," whispered Wilbert Bock. "They'll come in here and kill us." The radio operator was shaking. His face was white.

Wilbert Bock had been on the *Mayaguez* for 8 1/2 years, far longer than anyone else. A quiet, sensitive man, he liked to sit in the green leatherette chair in front of the main transmitter reading Shakespeare sonnets. Sometimes he even tried writing a little poetry, having taken a correspondence course from the Famous Writers' School in Westport, Connecticut. But Bock was no match for this bull of a man English.

English glanced down at the radio log lying on the counter next to Sparks's typewriter. The page was blank, though Sparks swore he had gotten out the first SOS on the 500 kilocycle band, even before the Cambodians came aboard.

"That's nothing," shouted English. "What'd you tell 'em. So they got your goddamn SOS and all they know is the *Mayaguez* is in distress at 9 degrees 48 minutes north and 102 degrees 53 minutes east. They don't know what the hell's going on."

Sparks sat staring at his new blue ITT key, his hands trembling.

"Call somebody," yelled English. "Break in on a working frequency."

Finally Sparks turned on the transmitter and tapped out a couple of feeble da, da, da, da's. Then he turned it off again "See," he whispered, "nobody answers."

English grabbed the mike on the single sideband. He didn't know how to use the big set, even though he had started out to become a radio operator on the GI Bill right after he got out of the Marines. "The dots and dashes drove me nuts," he always used to say. But the single sideband operated just like a telephone. "MAY-DAY, MAYDAY," he shouted into the mike.

"Be quiet. They're going to kill us," cried Sparks, half-trying to grab the microphone away.

"Keep your hands off," yelled English.

A Philippine ship picked up the SOS. English could hear the ship clearly. But he feared that the Filipino operator didn't really understand what he wanted him to do. "Contact the U.S. government. Call the American authorities," English shouted. He tried speaking Tagalog. His wife Cora, a wisp of a Filipina, about four feet eleven and about one-third English's weight, had taught him the native tongue. But even in Tagalog, he wasn't certain the message was getting through.

English raised another ship: an Aussie, he guessed from the radio operator's accent. The operator said he had heard English talking to the Philippine ship and had already relayed the SOS to his own office. But the Aussie refused to identify his ship or to confirm his nationality. This, too, made English nervous. He wanted to hear the *Mayaguez* plea for assistance go out on the air.

"Do it again," insisted English. "Call the American authorities. Call anywhere you can."

English heard the Aussie rebroadcast the SOS with the *Mayaguez*'s correct position.

"You may be the last English voice I hear for a long time," lamented the third mate as they signed off.

"Things can't be that bad, mate," said the Aussie.

It may have been his Viking heritage, or perhaps simply his superb physical fitness which he attended to about 2:30 every afternoon within the air-conditioned confines of his eight-by-fifteen-foot cabin. In any case, Jared Clifford Myregard, the trim, blonde, and blue-eyed thirty-three-year-old second mate, was the only man on the *Mayaguez* who would be instantly recognized as a seafarer. Myregard had just finished his daily workout—push-ups, chin-ups, jumps, knee-bends, and a mile of running-in-place—when the Cambodians captured the ship. Somehow while working up a sweat, he had failed to notice the gunboat pull along side, even though he occupied a starboard cabin. But when Myregard wandered out in his socks for his post-exercise cup of cold water at the companionway cooler, he heard the commotion. A pair of armed men in black pajamas were trying to herd the entire crew of the *Mayaguez* out on the starboard deck. Pirates? Viet Cong? Cambodians? He couldn't tell. He could only surmise that these black-clad men, whoever they were, had taken over the ship.

Jerry pulled on his sneakers and loped up the inside stairway to the bridge to find out what the hell was going on. Had they wandered off course? As second mate, he was the navigator. On his four-to-eight watch this morning he had drawn the trackline which the ship presumably was now following. He was a meticulous navigator. "When Jerry gives you a bearing," Captain Miller often said, "you know it's right." Miller planned to write a letter to Robert E. Fall, the company port captain in San Francisco, recommending Myregard for a chief mate's job on one of the Sea-Land ships.

Reaching the bridge, Jerry saw the situation. The captain and Burt Coombes were still handling the ship: calling out the compass headings and operating the ship's telegraph. And LaBue was at the

wheel. But they were prisoners. The commands were coming by
sign language from a short stocky man in black pajamas, who had
an AK-47 slung over his right shoulder. The ship was running
half-ahead, about 4.5 knots, following in the wake of a small grey
gunboat. From the lush green profile of the island ahead, he knew
it must be Poulo Wai. This morning, while laying down the trackline, he had vaguely recalled a story about a year ago of a Cambodian oil rig being chased away from Poulo Wai by the South
Vietnamese Navy. In any case, he knew both Cambodia and South
Vietnam claimed the island.

Jerry Myregard felt no panic, only rage at the sight of the four
armed men on the bridge. Ordinarily he considered himself a cool,
taciturn person. He made it a point never to reveal his moods,
staying clear of the petty shipboard disputes and not even socializ-
ing with the other men on the *Mayaguez*. In the officers' saloon he
rarely opened his mouth except to eat. And he did that sparingly
too, having disdain for all the pot bellies he had seen spawned by
the heaping servings and sedentary life at sea.

But when he saw the four armed men in the wheelhouse his first
instinct was to not submit to this act of piracy. He eyed the three
AK-47s and the rocket-launcher they were armed with. "You've
got two alternatives, Myregard," he said to himself. "Escape or
resist." He wondered if Captain Miller had considered resisting, or
turning tail and running when the men tried to board. He remembered the old Army axiom from his Fort Ord days: "Don't wait
for your captors to get organized. Attempt to escape immediately."

He studied the island ahead: really two islands, he remembered
from the chart, a pair of footprint-shaped atolls stepping out into
the Gulf of Thailand. The closest of the two atolls was about three
miles away. The gunboat appeared to be heading for the channel
between them, while the *Mayaguez* was bearing to the left, steaming on a course that would take it around the western tip of the
island.

The armed gang's commander, or whatever he was, gestured

angrily at the gunboat. It was clear that he wanted the *Mayaguez* to follow. "Too shallow," Captain Miller said shaking his head. "Too shallow. We'll run aground in there."

Jerry wondered if the pajama-clad little man understood what the captain was talking about. But the man nodded. Apparently he understood.

Jerry slipped out on the port wing. Most of the crew he had seen had already been herded out on the starboard side of the cabin deck. A couple more men in black were standing guard over them. He couldn't see anybody on the port side of the ship. It was deserted. "When we ease around the end of the island," he said to himself, "I could slip over the side without being seen." He studied the island again. "At this speed," he thought, "I've got about forty minutes to make up my mind."

FOUR
Seeds of Resistance

THE SEA SHALLOWED and paled, turning a milky aquamarine, as the ship, now starting the second hour of her seizure, crept around the western tip of Poulo Wai and there entered upon the greatest adventure of her life.

Four lives, counting all previous incarnations. She had been a war baby, of course, conceived as hull No. 114 at the North Carolina Shipbuilding Co. She was one of a fleet of C-2s slapped together from keel-laying to completion in a little over three months. On April 24, 1944 she was christened *White Falcon* by the War Shipping Administration and turned over to American Export Lines to operate in the North Atlantic Convoy Service. She was considered fast in those days. Fast enough, anyway, to keep from getting picked off by U-boats lurking around Halifax in the fog.

In 1947 Grace Lines picked her up as a war surplus bargain and rechristened her *Santa Eliana*. For the next twelve years she hauled machinery to Venezuela and brought back cork and bananas. But Grace had visions of pioneering a new invention in shipping—containerization—and decided to experiment with the *Santa Eliana*. But to do that the ship had to undergo surgery and she was sent off to the Maryland Shipbuilding and Drydock Corporation. Her hull was cut in two just forward of the deckhouse. A new 45-foot section was inserted, stretching her overall length to 504′1″. Then two flotation tanks, called sponsons, were welded to

her sides widening her in the beam to 74′2″. Finally, a second
bridge was tacked on for added height. Cranes replaced the booms,
and the five cargo holds were converted to container cells. All
primped for the latest trend in shipping, she immediately became
embroiled in a labor boycott and got stuck away in Baltimore to
rust. Grace finally gave up on the *Santa Eliana* and Sea-Land
Service, Inc. took over the ship and sent her to the Ingalls yard in
Pascagoula, Mississippi for more surgery. This time her container
cells were enlarged to accomodate the big new 35-foot boxes, which
when hooked up to a cab become the semi-trailers seen careening
around the world's highways. Sea-Land re-rechristened the ship
Sea (Her sister ship, the *Santa Leonor,* also acquired from Grace,
was named the *Land*) and put her on a gulf run to Puerto Rico.
As a friendly gesture to Puerto Rico she was renamed again, this
time *Mayaguez,* after the port city on the western end of the island
(sister ship *Land* became the *Ponce*). Finally in September, 1975,
the *Mayaguez* sailed out of New Orleans bound for Oakland and
the Orient and a new career in the China Sea.

Her new run in Southeast Asia—Hong Kong to Saigon to
Sattahip to Singapore—was soon altered by the swiftly changing
military situation. On April 21 the *Mayaguez* pulled away from the
new container dock in Saigon and started snaking her way down
the river to Vung Tau. "Next trip maybe I'll stay aboard and sail
to Hong Kong with you," confided the South Vietnamese river
pilot to Captain Miller. "You'll be more than welcome," answered
Charlie. But there was no next trip to Saigon. The city fell to the
Communists nine days later. And in the Gulf of Thailand, a border
dispute between the Thais and the new Khmer Rouge rulers of
Cambodia, was suddenly roiling the waters there. Several unarmed
Thai fishing boats had already been commandeered by the Khmer
Rouge. Even some big ocean-going freighters of various nationali-
ties had been fired on and stopped. But as it is not the custom of
the Defense Mapping Agency to issue Special Warnings to Mariners on anything so minor as this, the *Mayaguez* had not been

warned. Only forty-five such Special Warnings to Mariners have
been issued since the days of John Paul Jones. The last such Warning was issued at the time Haiphong harbor was mined. (A Special
Warning was issued for Poulo Wai on May 13, the day after the
Mayaguez was seized.) Anyway, news at sea always travels slowly,
and as the *Mayaguez,* now in the hands of its Cambodian abduc-
tors, rounded the western tip of Poulo Wai, there were two sound
sleepers aboard—Juan Sanchez and Alfred Rappenecker—still
oblivious to the fact that their ship had been seized.

Second Engineer Sanchez hadn't bothered to get up for lunch.
When he gets off watch at eight o'clock in the morning, he likes
to eat a big breakfast and then sack out until the oiler, Faria,
knocks on his cabin door at 3:45 in the afternoon. Right on schedule Faria banged on Sanchez's door. He might have told him what
had happened. But he didn't. No use gettin' the second all excited,
Faria thought. We'll give him the bad news when he gets down to
the engineroom.

Actually, Juan Pacheco Sanchez, a fifty-year-old Nicaraguan
from Corinto, had been getting bad news aboard ships just about
all of his seagoing life. Aboard the *Luxembourg Victory,* in Thailand where they had stopped to pick up a baby elephant and some
poisonous snakes for the San Francisco Zoo, he got word that his
brother had fallen off a train in Nicaragua and been killed. Later
he heard the news that the ship itself, renamed the *Pennsylvania,*
had gone down with all hands including some of his buddies. Then
there had been the time aboard the *Santa Adela* when Sanchez got
word that his sister had died of a brain tumor. And the two other
times when the bad news had followed him to sea: that his first
wife, Ramona, and then his second wife, Yelva, were divorcing
him.

Despite all this, Sanchez's wide mouth was usually turned up
in a smile, and his black eyes, even through tinted glasses, always
seemed to be laughing. Of all the deck and engineroom officers

aboard the *Mayaguez,* Sanchez was the best humored. "Give me the swingin' sirloin," he'd say to Omer the messman whenever braised oxtail appeared on the menu. Because he rarely ate lunch, he took bananas back to his cabin by the bunch. "I'm half-monkey," he'd say, grinning at Captain Miller who accused him of eating up all the ship's bananas.

When Faria banged on the second engineer's door, Sanchez was in a deep sleep. For a few minutes he lay languishing in his bunk. Then he pulled on his grey coveralls and stepped out into the companionway. There, he ran practically head-on into two armed men. I'm dreaming, Sanchez thought. My brain is still asleep. He stepped back into his cabin and closed the door. When he came out the second time, Electrician Salvatore Puntillo was standing there too.

"Who are these men?" asked Sanchez.

"Cambodians," said Puntillo. "They've captured the ship."

The Cambodians waved their rifles at Sanchez and Puntillo to get out on deck. "It's four o'clock," protested Sanchez pointing to his watch. "I've got to go to work." The Cambodians shoved the engineer and electrician up the stairs and out onto the starboard deck. Just about the entire *Mayaguez* crew had been assembled there. A third Cambodian, nervously fingering the trigger-guard of his AK-47, was trying to line everybody up. "My God, somebody's going to get killed," Sanchez said to himself. "I better try to go below."

"My friend," said Sanchez to the trigger-happy Cambodian, "I've got to go below." He pointed down to the engineroom. The Cambodian shook his head. So Sanchez waited. Five minutes later he approached another of the armed men and again pointed to the engineroom. "Please, my friend," said Sanchez, "I've got to go to work."

The second Cambodian shook his head. "No," he answered in English. But Sanchez persisted. He led the Cambodian into the companionway and pulled open the engineroom door. A blast of hot air hit the Cambodian's face and the deafening noise struck his ears. Sanchez never looked back. He stepped out onto the catwalk and headed below.

There was nothing unusual about the fact that Alfred J. Rappenecker, the third assistant engineer, was sound asleep and snoring in his cabin at four o'clock in the afternoon. A short beefy man with a big bulbous nose, he liked to eat a substantial lunch—a mess of spare ribs, say, with a side order of spaghetti—and then sleep it off. But on this day, because a fire and boat drill had been scheduled for 3:15, he ate light—two bowls of French onion soup with croutons, one of his favorite dishes, and climbed into his bunk.

At sixty-four, Rappenecker was the oldest man aboard the *Mayaguez.* Except for a few years ashore, when he and a friend owned a bar and grill in San Francisco, he had devoted his life to enginerooms—in every job from wiper to chief. He joined the *Mayaguez* on February 19. And many times since then Rappenecker said: "This is a good ship. She has a nice little engine. Not like the *Beauregard* where everybody is always drunk down below and the engine is a mess." But then, Rappenecker was very good natured, a fact he attributed to having a Spanish mother and a German father. Of course, he had a few peculiarities too. Rarely did Rappenecker ever go out on deck. "Sometimes I don't see that sea out there for a whole trip," he boasted. All he did was work, eat, and sleep, and read cowboy books.

This afternoon he had read for a few minutes and then dropped off to sleep, expecting surely to be jolted awake by the fire-alarm bell and ship's whistle at 3:15. A few minutes past four, hunger pangs woke him instead. He glanced at his watch: 4:05. It must be wrong, he thought. He looked over at his clock: 4:05. Then it hit him. Must be a power failure. Everything was so quiet. He pulled on his coveralls and walked down the companionway to the officers' mess. He knew Omer the messman always set the tables for supper at 3:30. But the white tablecloths were still folded up around the condiments. He looked in the refrigerator. The salads hadn't been made either. Pastrano the pantryman always made them before four. "What the hell's happening?" he asked himself. "Where is everybody?" He stepped out on the port deck. He hadn't seen the ocean since they left Hong Kong. It looked pale and the ship seemed to be coasting. Nobody was on deck either. "Jesus, the whole goddamn crew's disappeared." It reminded him of a war movie he had once seen in which a relief crew had to be flown out to a ship found drifting unmanned in the middle of the ocean. The original crew had mysteriously vanished, all except for one man. "That's me," he realized. "I'm the guy they left behind." Suddenly, he could visualize a whole new crew being delivered to the *Mayaguez* by helicopter.

Rappenecker had, in fact, been helicoptered off a ship once himself. In 1968 aboard the *Morgantown Victory* he had suffered his first heart attack. The ship was on a shuttle run between Saigon and Subic Bay, and fortunately a chopper could be summoned from Subic. They strapped Rappenecker into a vest with a big metal ring in back. "Then they picked me up with a meat hook," he claimed. Since then he has had more heart attacks. But now he carries a year's supply of nitroglycerine aboard ship with him.

He glanced at his watch: 4:10. "Too late for fire and boat drill," though he did recall one time aboard the *Mayaguez* when Captain Miller had delayed sounding the alarm until almost suppertime. "That's it," he decided, "everybody's at fire and boat drill." He walked to the starboard side on his way up to lifeboat No. 1. Through the open door he saw a young boy in black with a bando-lier of ammunition slung diagonally across his chest. The boy flicked the barrel of his gun, motioning for Rappenecker to step forward and join the rest of the *Mayaguez* crew lined up along the starboard railing.

Every few minutes now, Captain Charles Miller would feel another tap on his shoulder. It was the Cambodian ensign's—he had finally concluded the man was an ensign—signal for them to step back into the chartroom. It had become a ritual. Each time the ensign would point to the chart where he had penciled in the anchor. And each time Charlie would say: "Too shallow." But now they had rounded the western tip of the island and the ship was coasting in deep water. Jim Newman, the chief mate, was waiting on the fo'c'sle head to break out the anchor. He couldn't stall much longer, Charlie realized. Though ever since Dave English had come back up on the bridge and reported that he personally had gotten the SOS out to two ships, Charlie half-expected to see a wave of American bombers come swooping in from Thailand. He wanted to delay, as long as possible, letting go the anchor.

Charlie walked out onto the starboard wing to study their position. On the densely vegetated island he could now see a tower. From the sea side only the top was visible, though you would have to know it was there to pick it out. From that tower, he realized, the Cambodians probably saw the *Mayaguez*'s black hull and wisp of smoke from fifteen miles away. "The little shitheads," he said to himself. "They were probably sitting there for an hour waiting for us."

He could also now see the gunboat speeding around the other end of the island, doubling back towards the *Mayaguez*. But instead of continuing on that course, it veered off to the beach. He watched it cast out its anchor, then swing its stern around to a little bamboo jetty protruding from the beach. Soon he could see a line of black ants, or so they appeared, streaming onto the stern of the gunboat. More armed guards for the *Mayaguez*, he guessed.

Ordinarily Charlie would have telephoned up to the fo'c'sle head to let go the anchor. But before when he had reached for the engineroom telephone, the Cambodian ensign had waved the muzzle of his AK-47 in his face. Not menacingly. Just earnestly enough to make the point. From the starboard wing he yelled down to the bosun who relayed the yell to the chief mate up on the fo'c'sle head. "Just give me one bell for each shot of chain," Charlie had in-

structed Jim Newman the chief mate before he had gone up to the
bow. He heard the first bell and glanced at his watch: 4:14.

But the *Mayaguez* no sooner had her hook down—4 1/2 shots,
Charlie had ordered to give her plenty of scope—when the Cambodian ensign started on his old refrain.

"Go Ream," he said. "Go Ream, wharf number two."

Charlie knew the course the ensign wanted him to follow into
the Baie de Ream or Kompong Som. The ensign had marked in
on the chart. It looked like the channel was probably marked with
buoys, even though they did not show on the chart. But Charlie
could see the small black appendage on the chart, which he assumed was wharf number two. It was sticking out from Kompong
Som. But goddamn it, he didn't want to go there.

"Too dangerous go Ream," he said. He led the Cambodian
ensign over to the radar on the starboard side of the wheelhouse.
Then he flipped it on. "See, no picture," he said. "Broken." True,
the *Mayaguez*'s radar had conked out that morning and the green
illuminated screen was blank. "Go Ream in dark, very dangerous,"
Charlie said. "Go on reef."

The ensign didn't appear convinced. He's beginning to get
jumpy, Charlie thought. The ensign tapped the barrel of his AK-47
and pointed to containers stacked on the forward deck.

"No guns in there," Charlie said. "No guns. No ammunition
on ship."

Once in Kobe almost forty years ago when Charlie had been
bosun's mate on the old *President Pierce,* the Japs had held their
whole crew virtually prisoners for ten days, while they went over
the ship, searching for arms and ammunition. But that was during
the Sino-Japanese War and the *President Pierce* was bound for
Shanghai with a load of trucks and howitzers. The Japs finally
stripped the ship and let the crew go. Christ, he thought, if they
take us into Kompong Som and comb through 274 containers,
we're going to be here a couple of months.

"No guns, no ammunition, no electronic equipment. Nothing

but general cargo," Charlie repeated. But the ensign's face remained as blank as the radar screen.

Once again the ensign came on with his refrain. "Go Ream," he ordered. Charlie could see that he was now getting extremely agitated.

Finally, Charlie yelled up to the bosun to start heaving the anchor. He could hear Jim Newman give him the bells in reverse for each shot of chain coming up.

He decided to have one more go at the Cambodian ensign. "Too dangerous," he said again. "Ship go on rocks." This time he pointed to the bow of the *Mayaguez* and tried to convey the picture of a shipwreck with his hands. Then he flipped on the radar switch a second time. "No picture, see. Too dangerous go Ream in dark," he said.

At last the ensign relented. "OK," he said.

"Let go the anchor," Charlie shouted to the bosun, and again the message was relayed to the chief mate on the bow. Charlie checked his watch. It was now 4:55. Gunboat 128 was just coming back from the beach with a fresh load of armed guards, twenty more men all in the same garb: black pajamas, headbands, sandals, with the same assortment of weapons: AK-47s, M-79 grenade-launchers, and shoulder rockets. This batch looks even younger than the first, Charlie thought. He watched them come up the pilot's ladder and fan out over the ship. One group headed for the bow. Another group went to the fantail. And about eight more men suddenly appeared on the bridge.

One of the Cambodians looked ridiculously young, Charlie thought. Eleven or twelve maybe. The boy had a shaved head and Charlie instinctively reached out to rub it. As his hand moved over the bristly scalp, he said: "You babysan. Me papasan," forgetting for a second that his young captors were not Japanese. But the boy grinned. The rest of the Cambodians suddenly grinned too. Even the ensign showed a flicker of a smile. This might not exactly call for a party, Charlie thought, but I might as well make these fellas feel at home. Almost as if he had been summoned for the occasion, Omer the messman appeared on the bridge.

Usually the first thing Captain Miller would say by way of a greeting to Omer the messman was: "Omer, how's your camel?" It was their private joke, and Omer would always answer: "He's fine, Cap." This time the captain merely said: "Omer, go down to the slop chest and break out some of those Camel cigarettes. Get some apples and oranges, and tell that lazy steward to get off his ass and mix up a bucket of Kool-Aid and bring it up here."

Munasser Thabit Omer, thirty-one, the small, alert, curly-headed messman from South Yemen, had already been passing out apples and oranges to the Cambodians in the pantry below. Omer was quick to adapt to any new situation. The seizing of his ship was no exception. "These are children," he had told himself, "even though they all carry guns. They don't know nothing. If I'm nice to them maybe I'm going to live."

Omer, who is from South Yemen and who serves the officers' saloon, and his cabin-mate Kassem Saleh, who is from North Yemen and serves the crew mess, had joined the *Mayaguez* together in Oakland in October. In port, at least in those ports at which they didn't remain aboard ship, Omer and Kassem knocked around together, though Omer liked Sattahip because "nobody bothers nobody," and Kassem liked Subic Bay for the same reason other sailors did. It was wide open. Both messmen, though, went to sea for one reason, it was a job where you could save practically all of your earnings. For Omer this had become imperative. Married at age thirteen, he only had one wife and two children. But he had accumulated eighteen other family members back home in South Yemen, dependent on his support. "We have little bit farm," he explains, "with little bit coffee trees and little bit wheat. Not enough to live on."

Omer surveyed the strange scene on the bridge, and he could see why the captain wanted the apples, oranges, Kool-Aid, and

Camel cigarettes. There were a lot of Cambodians with guns standing around the wheelhouse, and Omer assumed if Captain Miller
was nice to them, maybe he'd live too. But he also knew precisely
what was going through the captain's mind. The Camel cigarettes
were the slowest sellers in the slop chest. In fact there was one case
that must have been there a year. They were stale. And as for the
steward, Ervin Anderson, Omer knew he somehow rubbed the
captain the wrong way. Actually, it was the chief and the steward
who were always feuding. But the captain got dragged into it. A
valve broke in one of the steward's reefer boxes. Every time he
opened it and hot air got inside, the temperature shot up. The
steward kept bugging the chief to fix it. But the chief said he needed
a new valve, which he didn't have on board. "All my ice cream is
melting," Anderson kept yelling. Finally, this morning the captain
couldn't stand listening to the argument anymore.

"All you ever worry about, Anderson," exploded Captain
Miller, "is your ice cream getting spoilt. When we get to Singapore
I'll buy you enough damn ice cream so you can take a bath in it,
if you'll quit your damn crying."

Omer nodded obediently to the captain. His eyes had a twinkle
and blink to go with the nod, that said: "Yes, sir, just as fast as I
can get it." That's the way he served his meals. It rarely took Omer
more than thirty seconds to rustle up an order, and that included
the time it took the food to come up on the dumbwaiter from the
galley below.

In a few minutes Omer the messman was back on the bridge
loaded down with the Camel cigarettes, and the apples and
oranges. He spread the open cartons around the wheelhouse. The
Cambodians helped themselves, a pack at a time. The boxes of
wooden matches made an even bigger hit. They kept going back
for more matches. They grabbed the apples and oranges too, but
when the water bucket full of orange Kool-Aid arrived, the Cambodians refused to taste it.

"They think it's poisoned," said the captain. Omer watched the old man pick up a styrofoam cup and fill it with the bright orange liquid. "Very good," he said quaffing the Kool-Aid and rubbing his stomach. "Very good." The captain poured another cup and handed it to the second mate. Omer watched Mr. Myregard do the same thing, drink the Kool-Aid and rub his stomach. Finally, the Cambodians joined in. In ten minutes the whole five-gallon bucket was dry.

"Go back down and fill it with ice water. I think these fellas are getting a little friendlier," Omer heard the captain say.

As an ex-Marine, Third Mate Dave English was struck by the growing laxity of his captors. He sneaked a sidelong glance at the young Cambodians lounging around the wheelhouse. Two of them were now sprawled out asleep on the starboard wing, their AK-47s laying on the deck next to them. "They're getting pretty sloppy," English said to himself. "All except little beady-eye over there, perched in the chair behind the radar with his gun resting on his lap."

English had formulated two objectives. He wanted to appear friendly so the Cambodians would relax in his presence. He wanted them also to become accustomed to his roaming around the ship, doing things the captain hadn't been allowed to. So he went below and picked up some more apples and oranges for the Cambodians. Then he picked up the phone to the engineroom and started talking. He wanted to see if the Cambodians would let him get away with it. They didn't stop him. "I'm an innocent civilian," English kept telling himself. "It's not as if I was still a Marine." But as a Marine in Vietnam he had never worried about being captured. He remembered how he used to sit up on top of his bunker at night smoking cigarettes, and in his mind at least, taunting the Viet Cong to come get him. "But then I was young and had a gun," he thought. "But maybe I can get a gun today."

English walked out to where Jerry Myregard was standing on

the port wing. He and the second mate had flown out together to join the *Mayaguez* in April. Burt Coombes had come on the same plane. Myregard had impressed him right from the start. "He's a smart, tough little guy."

"Jesus, Jerry," English said. "We got to figure some way to get out of this."

"I was thinking the same thing," answered Myregard. The two men decided to split up and canvass the ship. "Let's find out where these bastards are and what they're armed with," said English.

English went to the main deck and started on the fantail. He discovered a Cambodian stretched out on a cot. He picked up the man's M-79 grenade-launcher and examined it. The sleepy Cambodian didn't object. "I could sure raise hell with this little baby," English thought.

He walked the length of the ship to the bow. Up on the forepeak he found a half-dozen Cambodians. They had their AK-47s slung over stanchions. "When it's dark," English thought, "we could grab these bastards and throw them overboard." The only thing that worried him was the gunboats. A second gunboat, number 126 painted on its bow, had tied itself off the stern of the *Mayaguez*. "Well, they can't fire their rockets from so close in," he decided. "They'll blow themselves up. Anyway, maybe the gunboats will go back to shore tonight."

Before he completed his tour of the ship, English stopped in at the radio shack to find out if another ship by chance had tried to contact the *Mayaguez*.

"How goes it, Sparks?" he asked. Before Sparks could answer, the door opened and a Cambodian peered inside. English swung the door shut in the man's face.

"He'll come back here and kill us," cried the radio operator.

"Don't worry, Sparks. They're probably going to kill us anyway," said English.

Back up on the bridge English told Captain Miller what he had

found on his tour of the ship. "I think we could take these bastards," English said. "Throw them overboard, then slip the anchor
and make a run for it."

The old man didn't say anything. But he eyed English apprecia-
tively. The hulking ex-Marine was a good man to have aboard in
a situation like this.

"At least he seems receptive," English thought.

Down below the *Mayaguez* had taken on something of a carni-
val atmosphere. The Cambodians had discovered the hot and cold
running showers. Once they got checked out on how to use them,
they took turns frolicking under the jets. One man held all the
guns, while the others stripped off their black pajamas and jumped
in. The flush toilets were a novelty too. But the Cambodians insisted on standing on the seats. A hearts game had gotten under
way in the crew mess. The Cambodians stood gawking at the game,
gnawing away on apples and oranges. After a while they dug into
the big vat of steamed rice the cooks had prepared for them. For
some reason, they wouldn't touch the mashed potatoes.

In his cabin, First Engineer Vern Greenlin sat down and started
writing a diary for his friend Fred Cochrane, editor of the *Mountain Messenger* in Downieville, California. Maybe Fred can scoop
the world, Greenlin thought. If he isn't over in the St. Charles
Saloon getting boiled when my story arrives.

"Well," began Greenlin. "I don't know what's going on, but
we've been captured by Cambodia."

When the Cambodians first came aboard, Able-Bodied Seaman
Gerald Bayless may have been the coolest man on the *Mayaguez*.
He had been lying in his bunk reading when Gerardo Lopez came
in shouting, "They're shootin' at us. There's a ship out there shootin' at us."

Probably a routine inspection at sea, Bayless thought, and

resumed his reading. Later he stepped out into the companionway to try and strike up a conversation with one of the armed boarders. He wanted to determine for himself what the problem was. Bayless, who is blonde and curly-headed with a roguish Harpo Marx face, had good-naturedly handed the Cambodian a cigarette. They attempted to talk, but finally Bayless gave up. He never had been much good at making conversation, even with Americans, which is why he had quit the garage business in San Francisco and gone back to sea. "It was being nice to the customers that bugged me," Bayless always said.

When it came time for his watch—the eight-to-twelve—Bayless went up to the wheelhouse. The captain had given orders that he wanted the wheel turned fifteen degrees to the right and fifteen degrees to the left every few minutes to keep it loose, even though the ship was at anchor. Standing by the wheel waiting to turn it again, Bayless could hear the captain and second mate talking out on the port wing. He thought he heard the second mate suggest that the crew of the *Mayaguez* might be able to seize the ship back from the Cambodians.

"Bayless," the captain suddenly called out. He stepped out on the port wing to find out what the old man wanted. The sea had turned to glass and the molten glow had gone out of the sky. The deepening dusk accentuated the furrows in Captain Miller's face. He seems agitated, Bayless thought.

"Bayless, tell me," the captain said. "Is the crew talking about taking over the ship?"

"That would be suicide, sir," answered Bayless. "Nobody's talking about trying a crazy stunt like that. There must be twenty-five armed men on the ship now."

The captain pointed to the stern. "But the gunboat's gone," he said. "Maybe it won't come back tonight."

Bayless felt confused. He wasn't sure whether the old man was advocating some kind of a counter-attack against the Cambodians, or was simply seeking out one crew member's opinion. He was glad when the captain said: "OK, Bayless, go on back in the wheelhouse."

When Bayless got off the helm he hurried downstairs. English, the third mate, was just coming up. "Hey," said Bayless, "you know the captain and the second mate got some crazy idea about trying to take over the ship."

"I think we can do it," English said, and brushed on by.

Bayless rushed on down to the crew mess. The bosun, Jack Mullis, and a couple of guys were sitting around drinking coffee. "Jesus Christ," said Bayless. "The captain's gone crazy. He and the mates want to kill the Cambodians."

Captain Miller sat on the step out on the port wing wondering if the moonless night would ever end. "Goddamn gooks," he thought. "They won't even let me sleep." He was exhausted, and he felt old—battered and patched like his ship.

But ever since Charlie Miller quit going to school in the middle of the eighth grade, he had felt old. "My father was death on wives," Charlie always said in explaining his abbreviated childhood. "He had six wives and fifteen or twenty 'housekeepers,'" including one stepmother Charlie remembers as the "Heil Hitler Mrs. Schultz." With each new lady of the house Charlie was left to look after himself, until he finally ended up a ward of the court and was sent to live in Cary, Illinois with a man by the name of Johnny Hertz. Hertz owned the Yellow Cab Company in Chicago; later, with a group of associates, he organized the Hertz Drive Yourself Corporation which became Hertz Rent A Car. He also owned polo ponies and racing thoroughbreds, so Charlie, who at fifteen weighed ninety-eight pounds, found himself exercising both. The next thing he knew, he was racing at tracks like Washington, Arlington, and Sportsmen's Park in Chicago against jockeys like Johnny Longden, Earl Sande, and Jimmy Markham. His mounts were not usually the best. One horse crushed him under the inside rail and he had to have a silver plate put in his head. But he also had winners: a little mare called Butter Beans whom he booted home in the Cuban Grand National Handicap at Oriental Park in Havana, and Guy Frasier, known as the "King of the Half-Milers," though he would sometimes get the bit in his mouth and run forever. Charlie rode in Cleveland, New Orleans, and Tanforan, California, where they caught him one afternoon with a hypodermic needle in his hand. The owner was desperate. "Today you've got to win," he told Charlie, who instead found himself banned from racing, and washing dishes aboard the *President Hoover*. After one round trip between Los Angeles and San Francisco Charlie told the steward: "I'm not cut out to be a bus boy for a bunch of sailors," and he signed on the *President Coolidge* as an ordinary seaman. Thirty or forty ships later he ended up on the *Mayaguez*. By now he had sailed as a master for many years, but suddenly sitting out on the port wing looking up at the tropical star-filled sky, he wished he didn't bear that responsibility. "Not, at least, as a goddamn prisoner on my own ship," he thought. Right now the Cambodians might seem friendly enough. But he knew that any minute they could start pushing the crew around and belting them with their gun butts.

But it was a couple of his own crew members who were beginning to worry him more. "This Marine of mine. He may be fat but he's a powerful sonofabitch," Charlie thought. "If he can talk a couple of sailors into helping him, he might try throwing all the gooks overboard."

Charlie jumped. Somebody was shaking him. He looked up and saw the Cambodian ensign silhouetted against the sky.

"Go sleep," said the ensign. He escorted Charlie down to his cabin so he could go to bed.

FIVE

From Poulo Wai to the White House

"WE'VE GOT A LITTLE CRISIS," said President Ford. "I don't know why it is, but these crises always seem to occur on Monday." Standing in the soft light of the Oval Office graciously greeting his morning visitors, Gerald R. Ford's casual manner seemed to belie his words. He looked fit and relaxed after a weekend of golf, tennis, and swimming.

The president's day, as usual, had begun at 5:30 with the morning papers, though he was not then made aware of the chain of events which had taken place during the previous two hours. A Mr. John Neal of the Delta Exploration Company in Jakarta, Indonesia, had picked up a Mayday from an American merchantman named the *Mayaguez*. The message stated: "Have been fired upon and boarded by Cambodian armed forces at 9 degrees 48 minutes north and 102 degrees 53 minutes east." Mr. Neal finally gave up trying to reach the ship and telephoned the U.S. Embassy. The U.S. Embassy in Jakarta relayed the message to Washington, where it was finally received in the Situation Room, the muted, ochre-carpeted electronic center down in the basement of the White House, which has been the focal point for information on any ongoing crisis involving the president of the United States, since the Bay of Pigs.

It was 7:40 A.M. when President Ford was first made aware of the *Mayaguez*'s capture. Every morning, except Sundays or when he is out of town, the president receives an intelligence briefing by Lieutenant General Brent Scowcroft, deputy assistant to the president for National Security Affairs, assisted usually by David Peterson from the CIA White House support staff.

General Scowcroft, a small wiry West Pointer, with the balding, high-domed head of a professor (which he has, in fact, been), deftly sketched out the only skimpy details which were then available about the ship. The *Mayaguez* had been fired on and boarded by Cambodians, and was reported being taken into Kompong Som. There had been two previous incidents in the same area during past eight days. On May 4, a South Korean vessel, the *Masan Ho,* had been chased and fired on, one of its cargo holds being damaged by a shell. On May 7, a Panamanian vessel thought to be named the *Unid* (though later it was discovered that "unid" was simply the Navy abbreviation for "unidentified") had been seized, held for twenty-four hours and then released.

The briefing by General Scowcroft lasted twenty minutes. "My feeling is," said the president, "if they are going to take control not only of the ship, but of the personnel, it is a serious matter." He asked the general to keep him informed during the rest of the day.

At 9:23 Henry Kissinger arrived at the Oval Office, and seven minutes later he and the president were joined by General Scowcroft. It was decided then to call a National Security Council meeting for noon. "Things were still not entirely clear," said the president. "But I guess I was hoping that the best would take place, and not the worst. I fully understood that this was a very serious matter. At the same time I was hoping that the Cambodian government would, after they got the ship, release it."

At five minutes past noon, the National Security Council meeting got under way. The members filed into the Cabinet Room for the emergency meeting: Henry Kissinger, James Schlesinger, William Colby, and General David Jones, the Air Force chief of staff, substituting for General Harold Brown, who was away visiting NATO headquarters in Brussels.

At this meeting the president of the United States was governed by old feelings. During the Vietnam war, as the minority leader of the House he had always called for stronger responses rather than weaker responses. If there were going to be more actions like the seizing of this unarmed American ship, then the only way to effectively deal with them was to act decisively on the first one. "In Congress," recalled Ford, "I didn't have the final responsibility." Now he did.

In his mind, the ship at this moment lost somewhere out there in the darkness of night in the Gulf of Thailand, had become a symbol. The fate of the *Mayaguez* could become entangled in questions confronting U.S. foreign policy in Asia, or for that matter, all over the world. In Thailand, the Philippines, and South Korea, the U.S. was already being sharply criticized for its lack of resolve following the hasty helicopter evacuations of Phnom Penh and Saigon. In Europe where he would soon be visiting, President Ford knew he would be called on to reassert U.S. fortitude to his NATO allies.

The National Security Council began with the secretary of state arguing that what was at stake went far beyond the capture of an American cargo ship. The president quickly started asking questions. Where were the crew members? What men and equipment were available to respond to the situation? If the Cambodians had already interfered with South Korean and Panamanian ships, did they indeed have something special up their sleeve for the Americans?

The president talked about the *Pueblo* affair: "How it was similar in some respects," he said, "and different in others." "It was a benchmark," he believed, "from which they could proceed." The meeting lasted for forty-five minutes. The president made several decisions. He instructed Henry Kissinger to seek diplomatic assistance from the People's Republic of China in an effort to persuade the Cambodians to release the crew and the ship. This overture was to be made on two fronts: Huang Chen, chief of the Chinese Liaison Office in Washington, was to be summoned to the State Department, and given a message by Undersecretary Robert Ingersoll, with a request to relay it to Phnom Penh. At the same time, instructions to enlist Chinese assistance in freeing the ship and crew were to be transmitted to George Bush, the U.S. liaison chief in Peking.

"Again," said the president, "I wanted to be hopeful, but I also knew we had to make contingency plans in case the diplomatic initiatives were unsuccessful. At that meeting I told the Defense Department to start the movement of ships, to undertake the aerial surveillance, and to find out whether the crew was on the ship. Or first, where the ship was. We didn't know where the ship was at that time."

Accordingly, several specific military actions were initiated. The Third Marine Division on Okinawa was alerted and 1,100 Marines were ordered flown to Utapao Air Base in Thailand. The P3 Orion reconnaissance planes based in the Philippines, but sometimes refueling in Thailand, were ordered aloft to locate the *Mayaguez* and to keep it under constant surveillance. The aircraft carrier *Coral Sea,* bound for Australia for the second time in a month, was again ordered to reverse its course and head for the Gulf of Thailand. The carrier had first gotten under way to help Australia celebrate the anniversary of the Battle of the Coral Sea, only to be ordered back to aid in the American evacuation of Saigon.

None of the National Security Council decisions were publicly disclosed. Instead, White House Press Secretary Ron Nessen issued a brief statement: "We have been informed that a Cambodian naval vessel has seized an American merchant ship on the high seas and forced it to the port of Kompong Som. The president has met with the National Security Council. He considers the seizure an act of piracy. He has instructed the State Department to demand the immediate release of the ship. Failure to do so would have the most serious consequences."

Henry Kissinger then ordered a complete clampdown on State Department briefings of newsmen. His stated reason: "to let diplomacy run its course," was only partly correct. The president wanted it known that he personally had taken command of the crisis. State and Defense were to play supporting roles. As if to emphasize this point, Kissinger flew off to Missouri immediately following the National Security Council meeting. He had scheduled a series of speeches and press conferences around the country, part of the administration's campaign "to put Vietnam behind us."

The president followed a light schedule for the rest of the day. In the Oval Office he met with five ladies who had been named "International Women of the Year." He then spent the rest of the afternoon in conferences with his staff. The president invited options from his advisors, weighed them carefully, proposed new options of his own, and then selected the course of action which was to be taken.

At eight minutes past seven the president returned to the White House residence to have dinner alone with Mrs. Ford. At 10:29 P.M. he talked to General Scowcroft again. The telephone conversation terminated at 10:32. Then the president went to bed.

Commander Jim Messegee, thirty-seven, a Navy pilot with 5,000 flying hours and the good looks of a movie star—reddish brown hair, piercing blue eyes, and a carefully groomed moustache —had taken over as skipper of the Philippine Air Patrol Group on April 23. He had barely settled in at Cubi Point Naval Air Station, part of the Navy's sprawling Subic Bay complex, when word was flashed on April 30 to get all the Americans out of Saigon. For Messegee it was a grueling beginning. His group's mission was to provide the aerial surveillance—"Reconnaissance has another connotation," he explains—for the Seventh Fleet, which had assembled one of the greatest armadas in American naval history, off the Vietnam coast.

Now, on May 12, less than two weeks later, Messegee was sitting tanned and relaxed behind his desk. He glanced out the window at the crisscross of sun-baked concrete runways. The new desk job was challenging enough, but he missed the flying. He also missed his family, especially late in the day when he was getting ready to leave. Marlene and their three sons, Tim, Tom, and Todd, were back home in Honolulu.

The telephone interrupted Jim Messegee's reverie. It was OP-CON, the Operations Control room upstairs. They had been put on alert. An American merchant ship had been seized off the Cambodian coast. Messegee glanced at his watch: 1130 Zulu. Since Air Patrol operations frequently spanned different time zones, and were conducted on Greenwich mean time, Messegee just naturally thought in terms of Zulu, or simply Z as he called it.

Messegee had two squadrons under his command: the VP 4 "Skinny Dragons" and the VP 17 "White Lightnings," representing ten aircraft and 400 men. The planes, all P3 Orions, were four-engine turbo-props not unlike the old Electras, except they had been packed solid with electronic equipment in place of seats. Each plane carried a twelve-man crew, including three pilots. That way, on the prolonged twelve-hour aerial surveillance missions, most of which consisted of searching for underwater subs, the pilots could switch off flying and sack out in the triple-decker bunks back in the tail. On line at Cubi Point there was always one Ready Alert Bird prepared for take-off. The pilot of the Ready Alert Bird this particular afternoon was Lieutenant Jim Larkins.

"Call Larkins," ordered Messegee. Then he bounded out of his office and up the stairs to the OPCON room.

At the briefing in the OPCON room, Messegee estimated the flying time to Poulo Wai—the island from where the seized ship had sent its SOS—as 2 1/2 hours. Figuring a 5-hour round trip and a 1-hour spare fuel supply, that meant the surveillance plane could spend 6 hours on station, assuming it shut down one engine once it got there.

Within a few minutes Jim Larkins and his Ready Alert Bird were airborne. By 1430 Zulu, or 10:30 P.M. at Cubi Point Naval Air Station, Jim Messegee had received his first report on the *Mayaguez*. It was too dark for Larkins and his crew to eyeball the ship. But they could see the captured merchant vessel on their radar screens as a big target flanked by two little targets. The little targets they assumed to be a pair of Cambodian gunboats. And, as they also reported, with their eyes they could see orange tracers reaching up futilely into sky beneath them, and then falling down back to earth. The P3 Orion was out of reach of the two patrol boats' fifty-calibre anti-aircraft guns.

Four hours later Messegee relayed permission for Larkins to drop para-flares. As the brilliant seventy-million-candlepower lights ejected from the wing canisters and drifted towards the sea, the Gulf of Thailand in the vicinity of Poulo Wai was turned from night into day. There was no doubt now. The *Mayaguez*—black hull, white superstructure, and shiny steel containers—was there.

Still only a few miles off Subic Bay, from where Jim Messegee had sent his first P3 Orion winging off to Poulo Wai, Commander Bob Peterson stood on the bridge of the U.S.S. *Harold E. Holt* contemplating the problem of his destroyer escort's balky five-inch gun. The twenty-four–volt power supply in one of the control boards was malfunctioning. And though Peterson had once been a gunnery officer himself aboard the U.S.S. *Columbus,* he still hadn't been able to ascertain exactly what was wrong.

A short compact man with the first flecks of grey showing in his thick black hair, Peterson had been captain of the *Holt* since September, 1973. It was his first command and he wore the small round gold command-at-sea insignia pinned proudly above the right breast pocket of his suntan shirt. In four months he was due for reassignment. But he would be sorry to leave the *Holt*, which by peacetime standards was considered almost brand new, and, interestingly enough, the only ship in the U.S. Navy to be named after a foreigner. The ship had been under construction when Australian Prime Minister Harold Holt drowned. And President Lyndon Johnson decided to break precedent and name the destroyer escort after his friend and ally, who had supported the American cause in Vietnam so loyally.

During the evacuation of Saigon, the *Holt* had gone to the rescue of a fleeing Vietnamese Navy vessel, reported sinking in the South China Sea. Now in the fading afternoon of May 12, the *Holt* was running easily on routine maneuvers in the Philippine Sea. Bob Peterson, forty-one years old, squinted at the horizon through his contact lenses, very much the picture of a trim and vigorous Navy officer.

"There's a message, sir," said the signalman, and Robert A. Peterson and the *Harold E. Holt* set off at full speed for a position 9 degrees 48 minutes north 102 degrees and 53 minutes east, to try and locate a captured American merchant vessel named the *Mayaguez*. Peterson radioed back to Subic Bay that his main five-inch gun was out of order. He would just have to try and jury-rig repairs along the way.

Commander Mike Rodgers, captain of the guided missile destroyer *Henry B. Wilson*, had been a busy man for more than two months. From March 25 until April 17, when the U.S. government finally abandoned the Cambodian capital of Phnom Penh, the *Wilson* had played an important part in the evacuation operation named *Eagle Pull*. The destroyer had been stationed just off the Cambodian mainland, a few miles south of Kompong Som, or Sihanoukville as it was sometimes called, charged with providing "a defensive force against any air, surface, land-based, or subsurface threat which might endanger *Operation Eagle Pull*." The

Wilson's real job was to race around plucking American evacuees out of the sea if any of the helos got shot down. Fortunately, none were.

No sooner had Rodgers and the *Wilson* completed their Cambodian mission, than they were put on two-hour notice to raise steam and set off for the pending evacuation of South Vietnam, this one named *Operation Frequent Wind*. On April 30, the day of the final U.S. evacuation, Communist shore batteries began to shell the barges and transports moving off the Vung Tau peninsula. With her general quarters bells clanging, and her four boilers driving her through the water at thirty-one knots, the *Wilson* raced in between the beseiged evacuation vessels and the shore batteries, combing the beach with her five-inch guns. Twenty-six Communist shells splashed harmlessly in the water around the *Wilson*, the last shots fired at an American ship in the Vietnam war. Two days later the *Wilson* picked up a barge drifting helplessly with 2,000 refugees aboard.

On May 12, the *Henry B. Wilson* was steaming back to Subic from Kaohsiung, Taiwan's booming southern port, when it picked up a news broadcast. An unarmed American merchant vessel, the *Mayaguez*, had been boarded and seized right off the *Wilson*'s old Cambodian stomping grounds: Kompong Som. Commander J. Michael Rodgers was in his cabin at the time. He had a new book of two-move chess problems and had been pitting himself against the experts' plays. As an English literature major at Bowdoin and an intelligence specialist in the Navy, Rodgers liked to wrestle with problems of the mind—and at sea, he had found the chess board one of the best instruments for doing it. So on this evening he had failed to catch the news before he went to bed.

It was almost midnight when Mike Rodgers was awakened. Orders had come to proceed at full speed to the Gulf of Thailand. The *Henry B. Wilson* paused long enough in the Philippine Sea to take on full tanks of fuel from the U.S.S. *Ashtabula,* then turned her bow south. All four boilers were soon on the line, turning out 70,000 horsepower and driving the *Wilson* at thirty-one knots back to Kompong Som.

Tuesday, May 13

SIX

False Start for Sihanoukville

THIRD MATE DAVID CHRISTOPHER ENGLISH had too many things whirling through his brain to go to sleep. He tried his bunk briefly, went back up to the bridge, checked the radio shack, stopped in the officers' saloon, and returned to his cabin. What he found was tantalizing: Cambodians flaked out all over the ship, their rifles and rocket-launchers lying on the deck beside them.

"We don't need the whole crew, Burt," English said to the twelve-to-four third mate, Burt Coombes, who was up standing his watch on the bridge. "A couple of good strong guys, like you and me and Jerry and Sereno and we can take these guys. I've seen what they got. Grab a couple of their AK-47s and a grenade-launcher and we can push 'em right over the side."

Burt Coombes just shook his head. "Not me," he said. "I rather go to prison camp than end up a dead hero."

"Burt, maybe they won't bother taking you to prison camp," English answered. "Maybe they'll chop your head off instead. Then you won't be anything."

"I'll stick with the captain," said Burt. "Whatever he thinks we should do is all right with me."

"If they take us ashore, Burt, the captain's just one more guy. Suppose they march us down the main street of Sihanoukville and stand us up against a wall. What's the captain going to do? Go get us a lawyer?"

English had seen Sereno standing out on the port wing trying to converse with one of the Cambodians, so he went out there. Sereno was using a combination of pidgin English, Tagalog, and hand signals to try and make himself understood.

"This guy says he's been to Hong Kong, Saigon, Manila, and Singapore," Sereno said. "Says his name's 'Shawn Pike,' or something like that. We're going to Sihanoukville, he says, as soon as it gets light." Sereno, English discovered, had just taken "Shawn Pike" down to the crew mess for an early breakfast. Using the call letters: Mike India Lima Kilo, the man had made it understood that he wanted a glass of milk. "He must be some kind of a Cambodian radio operator," explained Sereno. "I let him make his own sandwich. Took three slices of everything: ham, cheese, liverwurst, salami, lettuce, and bread, and made himself a triple-decker." Then Shawn Pike had told Sereno that he felt sorry for him, which gave Sereno the impression the Cambodians planned to take them all into Sihanoukville and lock them up. "What do you think?" he asked the third mate.

English shook his mop of red hair. "We'll see," he said. Then he went down to the radio shack. Sparks was in a state of shock. There were three Cambodians sleeping on the floor. "Why don't you turn on the AM receiver and play 'em a little Cambodian bang-bang music," English said. "Maybe we'll catch the news." Damn if Sparks didn't do it.

Back in his own cabin again, English decided he'd better hide his valuables. No telling who'll come aboard in Sihanoukville. Anyway, like he told Burt, they'd probably all be marched down main street and made a spectacle of.

English had several personal belongings he didn't want to lose: the $800 mini-computer which he had bought with his own money to use as a navigation aid up on the bridge, his sextant, and a tape recorder. He lifted the plastic liner in his garbage can and put the computer under it. Then he threw some trash into the can. He pulled out the bottom drawer under his settee and hid the sextant behind it. The drawer wouldn't quite close, but it looked all right.

He climbed back in his bunk and tried to sleep. One last time, he decided. It was no good. He got to thinking how fluky it was that he ended up on the *Mayaguez*. He had just returned to Seattle from Masters, Mates, and Pilots School in Baltimore. On Monday, April 7, he dropped around to the union hall simply to see what was going on, not to get a job. But it was the first nice day in weeks in Seattle and the hall was empty. So they called the job and nobody else was there to take it.

Finally, he gave up trying to sleep. "Well, if we're going ashore," he told himself, "I better wear the right kind of clothes. We might be guests of the Cambodian government for a long time." He got out his jeans, long-sleeved shirt, high shoes, and a hat. His fair complexion burned easily. He filled the pockets of his jeans with vitamin pills. Then he walked down to the officers' saloon for an early breakfast.

Vern Greenlin was there. He and Vern discussed the best way to chew their food in prison camp to maximize the nutritional value. "In the Marine Corps," said English, "they told us to chew and chew and chew until it turns to water."

When he finally went back up to the bridge to begin his own eight-to-twelve watch, the action had started. English looked up and saw a four-engine Navy plane making lazy passes over the *Mayaguez*. On each pass, English noticed, the plane would lose a little altitude, until it swept past the *Mayaguez*, maybe 500 feet off the water.

"Well, he's sure found himself a hornets' nest," English hollered to Captain Miller. Forty Cambodians, who had been aboard the *Mayaguez* since early morning, blazed away with M-16s, AK-47s, and M-79 grenade-launchers, until they were all slipping and sliding around the deck on the spent cartridges. The two gunboats opened up with their twin-fifties. On the beach there were more fifty-calibre machine guns firing away. Some of the young Cambodian boys, English noticed, closed their eyes when they fired.

The Navy plane continued on out over the water and didn't return. "There's no way he could've flown through that shit-storm without getting hit," English exclaimed.

At 8:30 the Cambodian ensign ordered Captain Miller to start weighing anchor. At 8:44 the ship was underway, creeping at half-speed on a course of 022 degrees—headed in for Sihanoukville, or Kompong Som as the Khmer Rouge now called it. One of the gunboats led the way.

Juan Sanchez had come up from his four-to-eight watch in the engineroom and already finished breakfast, when the *Mayaguez* began moving northeast in the direction of the mainland. He had started rolling over the engine at four o'clock, expecting the ship would get underway at daylight. But he never got a bell. The half-ahead bell from the bridge came while he was at breakfast.

At nine o'clock, as he did most mornings, Sanchez got out his shortwave radio and tuned to Voice of America. The first news item was electrifying: President Gerald Ford had ordered the Cambodian government to release the *Mayaguez* and its crew, or face the consequences.

Sanchez ran out of his cabin looking for his two closest friends on the ship, Jack Mullis, the bosun, and Erv Anderson, the steward. The three of them were old-timers and liked to sit around at night rehashing the early union days. They frequently did favors for each other. Mullis would find Sanchez a piece of rope or canvas when he needed it in the engineroom. And Anderson was equally good about saving Sanchez a sandwich if he missed supper. The night before Mullis had mentioned that the only thing that worried him about their capture was his eighty-one-year-old mother's heart condition. He was afraid she'd have another coronary attack when she heard the news. Anderson said his wife also had heart trouble, and he feared for her too.

"Don't worry," Sanchez greeted his two friends. "We're going to get help now."

Half an hour later Sanchez gathered a group in his cabin to hear VOA's repeat broadcast. Newman, Myregard, Bock, and a few others, crowded around the second engineer's paint-stained green settee to hear President Ford's warning. "I'll just leave the radio on," thought Sanchez. "It seems to make everybody feel better."

What made Captain Charles Miller feel a great deal better at exactly eighteen minutes past one, was the realization that the *Mayaguez* and her crew were not headed into Sihanoukville, or Kompong Som, whichever you called it, but were going to anchor instead off Koh Tang, a dumbbell-shaped island, thirty-four miles away from the Cambodian mainland. All the way to Koh Tang, the Cambodian ensign had been sounding his refrain of the day before: "Go Ream! Go Ream, wharf number two!" And again today he had prodded the captain to keep pace with the Cambodian gunboat speeding ahead.

When he got the good news Charlie anchored in 100 feet of water about one mile north of the island. Immediately, five or six jet fighters—F-4 Phantoms, he thought they were—swooped down to strafe and rocket in front and back of the *Mayaguez*. So far all the planes had come on reconnaissance. These were firing. Plumes of water shot up into the air, and sent the Cambodians scurrying around the deck like rabbits, reminding Charlie of a ridiculous voyage he had once made as chief mate on the *President Taft*. Some 1,500 white rabbits had been loaded aboard the ship in Yokohama, destined for a medical research laboratory in Manila. Two days out to sea the rabbits succeeded in climbing out of their cages and the *President Taft* had white furry things scurrying all over the decks. Charlie and the sailors kept catching the rabbits and putting them back, only to have them escape again. Finally, the crew gave up and gave the rabbits the run of the ship.

Charlie worried that the explosions coming so close to the ship would scare the Cambodians out of staying. Nothing happened for a while. The Cambodian ensign escorted Charlie down to his cabin and made him open the safe. The $5,000 bundle with the rubber bands around it seemed very noticeable to Charlie, but the ensign ignored it and moved on to the file cabinets in Charlie's office. He didn't take anything, but he told Charlie to leave everything open. Then at about 4:15 he pointed to the captain and second mate and motioned towards the island. The ensign kept crossing and un-crossing his wrists, sign language which Charlie interpreted as meaning that he and Jerry Myregard would soon be handcuffed and taken over to Koh Tang for interrogation. Coombes was in the wheelhouse too, but the ensign didn't point to him. "It looks like you and me, Jerry, are going ashore," the captain said.

Chief Engineer Cliff Harrington was in his office lying on the settee trying to get some rest when he heard the rockets explode off the bow and stern. "Well," he said to himself, "something's going to happen now." He had a premonition that if things got bad aboard the ship, the Cambodians would take them ashore. "I better get ready," he told himself.

He shaved and showered and put on a long-sleeved shirt. The deck officers all had pretty good tans. But with his engineroom pallor, he knew he'd have to keep pretty well covered. When he finished dressing he went back down to the engineroom.

A few minutes later the third engineer, Al Minichiello, came down and said: "They're taking us off the ship." Right down the ladder behind him came Wilbert Bock, the radio operator. Har-rington could tell that Bock was agitated. An hour earlier he and Bock and English had been sitting in the officers' saloon having coffee when English popped off and said: "I'm not going like a lamb to the slaughter." English then described a hamlet near Hue which his Marine company had recaptured. "When we walked in there were nineteen Americans with their hands tied behind their backs and their heads chopped off," English said. "They were just sitting there. I had to go around and untie them." Bock turned white.

"What the hell, Sparks. You're as old as me," Harrington said.

"You've lived a hell of a big life already. Who's going to miss you?"

Harrington had already had those same thoughts about his own life. He had grown up in San Francisco. A pretty fair schoolboy athlete, he could have gone to San Jose State on a basketball scholarship. But he went to sea instead. "I never got the call to go to sea. I got the job," he always said. Yet it was the sea that repeatedly tugged against his family ties. Harrington adored his mother. On his first trip he bought her a canary in the Philippines. The captain of the ship, the *Meigs*, had bought a canary too, but Harrington's turned out to be a better singer. The whole way back across the Pacific, the captain kept trying to pull his rank and trade canaries. After the Leyte Gulf invasion, which Harrington joined in aboard the *Xavier Victory*, he arrived home and called his mother. His brother answered the phone, but knowing Cliff, didn't have the heart to tell him she was dead.

Harrington had five children of his own, and he quit the sea so he could be a father—first becoming a boiler inspector for the Royal Globe Insurance Company in Sacramento, then an agent in Stockton on the producing end of the business. "I'm doing pretty good," he said at the time. But right after his and Jeanne's twentieth wedding anniversary he walked out of the house and never went back. Fred Carter, his old World War II buddy from the *Evangeline*, took over the insurance agency. On the *Evangeline* Fred had been first engineer and Harrington second. They occupied suites *A* and *B* of the former luxury liner. One time, bringing a load of WACs up from Sydney to New Guinea, Fred hooked the fresh water line into their private showers to entice the WACs up to suites *A* and *B* to bathe.

When he left home, Harrington suddenly realized that he had let his engineer's license expire, so he went back to sea as a utilityman on the *General Walker*, and then sat for his license all over again. Last December he happened to drop into the Marine Engineers Beneficial Association to pay his dues when the chief's job on the *Mayaguez* came up. "I'm not too enthusiastic about keeping a thirty-one-year-old ship going," he said then. But he figured, "what the hell, the economy's slipping and they're laying up ships." So he took it.

Harrington watched the radio operator root around the engine-room like a scared chicken. Bock was poking around trying to pry up the steel floor plates and crawl underneath to hide. "Suppose those Navy planes out there bomb the ship and sink it," Harrington said. "What you going to do then, Sparks?" That didn't seem to faze the radio operator. He kept rooting around for a place to hide.

"For Christ's sakes, Sparks," Harrington yelled. Sparks was now way back in the shaft alley. "The Cambodians must know by now we got forty men aboard this ship. If only thirty-nine show up, they're going to come looking for you."

Harrington glanced up at the catwalk running across the engineroom forty feet above him. Black pajama pants were moving across the grating. Here and there he could see the glint of a rifle barrel. "They're coming down now," he hollered to his gang.

As he watched the armed men in black climb down the series of ladders, one thought clawed at his mind: "If they put us up against a wall or a bush somewhere and shoot us, I hope I've got the guts to stand there and face them without crying like a coward." Then the practical considerations of shutting down the plant —closing off the fuel-oil service pump and the burners in each boiler, and securing the sea suction valves—took precedent over thoughts of survival. Greenlin, Rappenecker, and Sanchez were all present. So were Conway, Faria, and Matthews. Harrington called out the orders before the Cambodians reached the bottom. The Cambodians pointed with their guns for everybody to go up. But first Harrington wanted to make sure feed water was pumping into the boilers so they wouldn't burn up. He stalled the armed men for a few minutes, then led his Black Gang—with Sparks in among them—up out of the engineroom. As he climbed the ladders he could feel his legs turn to Jell-o. "Come on, knees," he said, "don't quit on me now."

Before Dave English could change into the special clothes he had laid out to wear ashore, two Cambodians came into his cabin and grabbed him. They prodded him down the companionway with their gun barrels and pushed him out on deck. English tried to protest. He still didn't realize everybody was going ashore. The captain, second mate, and engineers, he knew were going. But the crew, he thought, was going to stay. "A ship without an officer," he always said, "was like a snake without a head." "I damn well better stay," he said to himself. Anyway, the idea of leaving his natural environment bothered English. It suddenly occurred to him that even though he and the crew had been prisoners of Cambodia for the past twenty-six hours, they had nevertheless been living in their own environment: sleeping in air-conditioned cabins, eating American frozen foods, listening to transistor radios, bathing in hot and cold running showers, and going about their jobs on deck or in the engineroom with all the things their company, unions, and country guaranteed. Suddenly, there they were, with guns in their backs being hauled away.

He looked down the pilot ladder and saw the captain and the second mate already standing on the deck of a fifty-foot grey fishing trawler pulled alongside the *Mayaguez*. Another fishing boat, he knew, was tied up on the port side of the *Mayaguez*. Then he glanced at the sky and saw the first jet flying straight at the *Mayaguez*. The Cambodians on the bridge and boat deck above him opened up with everything they had. Three more jets swept overhead. Again the Cambodians blazed away. Out on the starboard wing of the bridge, English could see a boy with a M-79 grenade-launcher letting go too. "Crazy kid," English thought. "That weapon's to stop slow, two-legged people with. Not one-thousand-mile-an-hour jet planes." His fingers itched to get hold of those grenade-launchers. "I could wipe out half these cats in one blast," he thought.

SEVEN

New Orders from Ford

AT 2:21 IN THE MORNING, President Gerald Ford was asleep when the telephone rang. It had been exactly three hours and forty-nine minutes since Lieutenant General Brent Scowcroft, his birdlike deputy assistant for National Security Affairs, had called to report that no further movement of the *Mayaguez* had been observed, the ship having anchored off Poulo Wai. Now the general was calling again, but with less felicitous news. Aerial surveillance planes had observed the ship proceeding towards the Cambodian port of Kompong Som.

At this early hour on Tuesday, the president became increasingly worried. "I've always had this thought," he said. "Here was a relatively new government, the Khmer Rouge, that had a reputation for being tough and uncompromising, with an attitude of, 'We're going to show the United States.' That was in the back of my mind, as their actions grew more definite and certain. They didn't search the ship and release it, but they took control and they kept it. I was confident that there was of necessity going to be a confrontation."

The telephone conversation lasted two minutes. Then the president went back to bed and to sleep.

At 6:22 the telephone rang again. This time it was Secretary Schlesinger. President Ford had been up for almost an hour and a half, having already clocked a mile on his exercycle and worked out with the leg-weights which are designed to strengthen his thigh and knee muscles. Both of the president's knees have been operated on: the left one after a football injury in 1932, and the right one in 1972 because it tended to lock when he went skiing. The president, being a morning person, had also read the *Washington Post,* with its front-page *Mayaguez* story, by the time the secretary of defense called.

Schlesinger had slightly encouraging news. The P3 Orion anti-submarine reconnaissance planes could now observe the *Mayaguez* at anchor off Koh Tang, a three-by-two-mile jungle island, thirty-four miles southwest of Kompong Som (actually, the ship had dropped anchor at 2:18 A.M. Washington time). The planes, the secretary said, had swept within 1,000 yards of the ship, and reported it to be dead in the water. The planes did, however, draw heavy machine-gun and small-arms fire, both from the ship and the island. One of the P3s took a bullet in its vertical stabilizer, but had returned to its base safely. The telephone call lasted eight minutes. But at 7:03 Schlesinger called back and he and the president discussed the *Mayaguez* for three more minutes. At 7:42 President Ford reached the Oval Office.

Seated in his shiny black leather swivel chair, with the South High School Football Club penholder placed squarely in the center of his desk in front of him, and the presidential and American flags behind him, President Ford was ready to commence his official day.

His first appointment, as usual, was with General Scowcroft, who today because Henry Kissinger was out of town, spoke for the secretary of state on all foreign and national security matters. This morning, of course, there was one overriding matter—the *Mayaguez.*

Scowcroft reviewed with the president the latest report that the *Mayaguez,* instead of continuing on its course into Kompong Som, had anchored off Koh Tang. With the ship thirty-four miles from the mainland, they reasoned that it might still be possible to prevent the Cambodians from taking their American prisoners to

Kompong Som. General Scowcroft left the Oval Office at 8:08, after it had been determined that another National Security Council meeting should be convened in about two hours.

Since the previous day's NSC meeting there had been an accident involving some of the troops mobilized to cope with the crisis. One suggestion made at the Monday meeting had been to land helicopters on top of the *Mayaguez*'s steel containers and retake the merchant vessel by force. The plan had not been rejected. But at the same time the "execute order" to do it had not been given. In the intervening twenty-two hours it was discovered that the only troops in the region trained in assault tactics for this kind of operation, were eighty Air Police stationed at Nakhon Phanom Royal Thai Air Base, or NKP as it's called. Orders had gone out to NKP to helicopter the Air Police to Utapao so that they would be ready to make the assault landing on the *Mayaguez*. But one of the helicopters containing eighteen Air Police and five crew members crashed shortly after take-off, killing all occupants. In one sense the *Mayaguez* had its first casualties. (Though, the following day the Pentagon, drawing on World War II and Vietnam casualty-counting procedures, ruled that the deaths were not officially *Mayaguez*-connected. The troops had not yet been committed to the operation.)

At 10:22 the National Security Council met. Kissinger, whistle-stopping through Missouri—from St. Louis to Jefferson City to Kansas City to Independence—was absent. This was taken as further indication that the president had personally taken command of the crisis, which he did not want publicly perceived as serious enough to force the secretary of state to interrupt his trip. From this meeting emanated the president's order that boats between Koh Tang and the mainland, as well as between the *Mayaguez* and the mainland, should be intercepted with minimal force. The president ordered that F-4 Phantoms, A-7 Corsairs, and F-III fighters from Utapao be used in immobilizing the Cambodian gunboats.

"We told the aircraft," said the president, "that they should use whatever legitimate means they could to head off either the ships to the mainland or vice versa. During the day I was to be given periodic reports on whether there was any movement." The NSC meeting ended at 11:17.

In initiating the air action he did, President Ford admitted drawing on his Navy experience aboard an aircraft carrier during World War II. As the president later explained, the *Mayaguez* was not his first crisis involving a ship dead in the water and vulnerable to attack. Said the president: "We were in one of the task groups that made the first strike against Taiwan in about April, 1944. Taiwan was under Japanese control, and when we went in and hit the island we were attacked by Kamikaze planes.

"That night two of our cruisers in the task force got hit, and we had to stay around there under continuous attack. One of the cruisers was dead in the water, and they had to get another cruiser and get a line over, and one cruiser started towing the other at about five knots.

"Here we were, three cruisers—one of them knocked so totally out of control they almost had to abandon ship—and five or six destroyers, only forty or fifty miles from Taiwan, which possessed ideal operating conditions for the Japanese land-based aircraft. The question was: How do you get the ship and the men far enough away so that they are out of range of the Japanese aircraft?

"The aircraft that kept the *Mayaguez* from being towed or moved into shore were not from an aircraft carrier. They were U.S. Air Force aircraft. But I could visualize the *Coral Sea,* with its flexibility, being a big asset. I must say I was glad we had an aircraft carrier that was around and could be used. It sort of helped to justify the need for aircraft carriers."

Following the National Security Council meeting the president met individually with seven members of Congress in what is referred to as one of the president's "congressional hours." The congressmen were not summoned to talk about the *Mayaguez,* but Representative Joe Waggoner, a Democrat from Louisiana, revealed later that Ford had said: "I've got a tough decision to make on the ship."

At 12:46 President Ford telephoned to Kissinger in Missouri to discuss with the secretary of state the possibility of setting a deadline for the Cambodians to release the *Mayaguez* (an ultimatum had even been drafted). The idea was eventually rejected because as Kissinger later revealed, "the risks were greater than the benefits, and the benefits were really domestic." An ultimatum, it was also feared, might have hardened the Cambodians' attitude even more. The telephone conversation ended after twelve minutes.

Newsmen traveling with Dr. Kissinger reported him to be in high spirits on the Missouri trip, which was interrupted by frequent phone calls, like this one from the president, and by the arrival of State Department couriers from Washington with new situation reports. One of the reports concerned the outrage expressed by Thailand's Prime Minister Kukrit Pramoj over the use of his country as a staging area for the 1,100 Marines flown in from Okinawa. Publicly Thailand did not want to take sides in the *Mayaguez* affair, and Kukrit gave the U.S. twenty-four hours to get the Marines out. Privately, though, Thailand had given its concurrence in bringing the Marines there in the first place.

Kissinger, who had seemed morose since the ignominious U.S. evacuations of Phnom Penh and Saigon, appeared to have regained his old ebullience. In Kansas City he pounded the podium with booming enthusiasm and proclaimed: "The United States will not accept harassment of its ships in international sea lanes." In private, too, he seemed remarkably buoyant. Asked by *Time* correspondent Strobe Talbott when he foresaw the incident ending, he smiled and said: "I know your magazine's deadline. I think we can meet it."

Not all of America's crises centered on Koh Tang, the minute, previously unheard-of island in the Gulf of Thailand. There was a crisis of another kind on Manhattan Island. At 2 P.M. the president met with New York Governor Hugh Carey and New York Mayor

Abraham Beame, who came to plead for federal assistance for the near-bankrupt city. (The president later rejected the request in a "Dear Abe," letter.) At 4 P.M. he presided over a meeting of his economic and energy advisors. At 5:30 P.M. the White House congressional liaison aides began telephoning leaders of Congress to inform them of the president's decision to use force, if necessary, to recover the *Mayaguez* and rescue its crew. The leaders were not told specifically that bombing and rocketing of the gunboats was contemplated. They were informed, though, that a message had been sent by way of Peking to the Cambodian government demanding that the ship and the crew be released, and notifying the Cambodians not to move the American ship or its crew from where they now were.

EIGHT

Dead in the Water

FOR A SKIPPER who's spent most of his seagoing days on passenger liners calling at the world's great ports, mused Charlie Miller, Koh Tang, Cambodia, is a hell of a place to end up in. The tropical island was pretty enough: white sand beach, blue shimmering water, lush green vegetation, and one hill. He could see a couple of dories pulled up on the beach. A lone man had been signaling vigorously from the shore to the fishing boat he was on, when they first anchored. And a few minutes before the dusky purple twilight had started playing tricks on his eyes, he thought he discerned some kind of a camp built in among the trees. Yet, so far, the only real evidence of activity on Koh Tang was the fountain of orange tracers spurting up from the island and searing the sky.

"Goddamn if I know what's going on," said the captain to his second mate Jerry Myregard. The two gunboats which had escorted their two fishing boats from the *Mayaguez* in to the island wheeled abruptly, sending a smooth, rounded wave rolling across the inlet, and headed back for the ship. "I thought you and me, Jerry, were going ashore to get interrogated. There's nothing here but a bunch of coconut trees."

Even the Cambodian ensign had disappeared. Charlie wasn't sure, but he thought the ensign had gone back to the *Mayaguez* on one of the gunboats. "Probably to pick up my five grand," he said to himself. The two fishing boats, with fifteen or twenty armed guards on them, had been left anchored gunwhale to gunwhale about 100 yards off the beach. "I guess we're going to stay here all night, Jerry," he said.

"Beats me, Captain," answered the second mate. Myregard had been peering apprehensively at the fringe of palmettos bordering the wide, crescent-shaped beach. "But I don't like the looks of it. These fellas are just trying to pacify us. Like I said last night, Captain, from what I hear the Khmer Rouge are great for taking people out and chopping their heads off."

The previous night, standing with Jerry Myregard up on the port wing of the *Mayaguez,* Charlie Miller had answered: "Let's just wait, Jerry. Let's wait and see what they're going to do. I don't want to get anyone in this crew shot and killed if we don't have to." This time he didn't say anything. Jerry, he could see, was edgy. And he'd already heard a few of the sailors grumbling. "Now what's the old man gettin' us into," he'd overheard Friedler the electrician say. And Bayless, he'd heard him mouthing off too: "This crazy skipper's gonna get us slaughtered." Maybe just the shit-disturbers in the deck gang, Charlie thought. But he didn't like to hear that kind of talk. It had a way of feeding on itself.

Darkness was settling over the water, expunging the last rays of light between sea and sky. Charlie looked back off the stern of the fishing boat. The two gunboats were purring along in tandem on their way back from the *Mayaguez.* One gunboat came alongside their fishing boat and tied up. The other tethered itself to the first gunboat's stern. Standing on the deck of the fishing boat, Charlie suddenly found himself being addressed in halting English by a member of the gunboat crew.

"No worry," said the man. "Cambodians no hurt you. Go back ship in morning." Charlie eyed the man, five feet one or two, he guessed. Several inches shorter than he was. Like all the other Cambodians, he was dressed in black pajamas. But he wasn't armed. "You captain?" asked Charlie.

"Driver," answered the man. Must be the quartermaster, Charlie thought. "Parlez-vous Français?" the "driver" asked, looking at Charlie hopefully.

"Hey, Pastrano," Charlie called out to the group of crewmen who had formed a semicircle around him to listen in on the conversation. "We need an interpreter." In his Louisiana French, boxer Willie Pastrano's father and the driver engaged in a nonstop exchange. Neither man, it seemed, could understand the other's French. Finally, Pastrano turned to the captain.

"He wants to know what's inside the locked rooms on the ship."

"Tell him, nothing. No guns, no ammunition. Just a bunch of clothes and personal belongings," said Charlie.

Pastrano had trouble conveying the captain's message. The driver kept shaking his head. "Tell him," said Charlie, "if he wants, we'll go back and unlock the doors. Then he can see for himself. But tell him the plant's dead. We got no electricity."

Charlie could hear a reconnaissance plane droning directly overhead. He had heard it before, faintly circling out over the water. Now from the sound, he guessed it was passing right over the island. Pastrano and the driver looked up. Then the black void behind the strip of white, separating the water from the island, exploded. Five or six machine guns—bigger stuff too—chattered and barked in unison. Orange tracers crisscrossed the sky. The acrid smell of gunpowder drifted across the water. "For Christ's sake, we're in the center of a goddamn war," he heard a voice say. Bayless's, he thought. But the firing sputtered and died leaving only the steady drone.

Charlie turned back to his pantryman and the gunboat's driver. "Tell him, Pastrano, if he wants me to I'll go back and open all the doors."

Again it took Pastrano a considerable amount of Cajun French, accompanied by gestures and signs, to get the captain's offer translated. The driver nodded.

"All right, you guys," Charlie called out, "everybody give me his keys." He circulated among the crew collecting keys until his pockets bulged. "Cliff," he said, coming to Harrington, "I can't hold the flashlight and run through all these keys to find the right one. You'd better come with me."

"Where are we going?" asked the chief.

Charlie turned and pointed to the driver. "Back to the *Mayaguez,*" he said, "to open up the rooms and show this young fella we don't have any guns or ammunition or electronic equipment."

Harrington and the captain had always gotten along pretty well. They took turns buying each other an expensive dinner at Hugo's or the San Francisco Steak House in Hong Kong after every trip. "Whatever you say, Captain," replied the chief.

Later, after the Cambodians had cleared all the other *Mayaguez* crew members off the smaller of the two fishing boats, and the captain and chief were on their way back to the ship, Charlie turned to Cliff. "You think I want you to come along just to show these fellas around the spaces between the machinery down in the engineroom?" Charlie asked. "Well, that's not the reason," he said before the chief could answer. "Hell, no, Cliff. In case I get shot, I want somebody there to get shot with me."

Their fishing boat came out of the crescent-shaped harbor, cutting a clean furrow through the dark glassy water. Between his own crew and all the Cambodians, Charlie guessed, there must have been eighty or ninety jabbering people scattered over that little flotilla back in the harbor. Now everything was quiet, only the throb of the diesel disturbing the night. He peered ahead into the blackness trying to pick out the *Mayaguez.* But he couldn't find her. Funny, he thought, how an old ship like that could become an overnight celebrity. Just before they had left the ship this afternoon, he had heard a news broadcast, and he had heard it wrong. "President Ford," he had understood the Voice of America to say, "has called on the United Nations Security Council to obtain the immediate release of the *Mayaguez.*" What the broadcast had actually described was President Ford's convening of his National Security Council to obtain the *Mayaguez*'s immediate release. But in any case, Charlie had no desire to have the whole world's attention riveted on his ship. All he wanted was to get himself and his ship the hell out of there.

•

The darkened ship now lying dead in the water off Koh Tang, had once before been the focus of an international crisis, though neither the world, nor for that matter her approaching captain and chief, could recall it. Like today, she had become a source of bitterness between the United States and another nation. Only then it was not Cambodia, but Venezuela.

On January 29, 1960—as the Grace Lines' *Santa Eliana*—she had set sail on her maiden voyage as a so-called seatainer for the port of La Guaira in Venezuela. More than 700 luncheon guests, city and state officials, had gathered at Port Newark to hail a new era in transportation. The *Santa Eliana,* it was claimed, as America's first fully containerized vessel in international trade, would help the United States to recapture its slumping position in world shipping.

From that day on just about everything went wrong. Arriving in La Guaira on February 2, Venezuela's Federation of Dock Workers wouldn't touch her. She threatened their livelihood as stevedores, they claimed. For twenty-two days the fully loaded ship, just as now, lay dead in the water outside La Guaira. The Venezuelan government tried to intercede, but without success. Grace Lines, which had sunk $3,500,000 into her remodeling and was now losing another $2,500 a day through idleness, refused to seek State Department assistance for fear of setting off a full-blown international dispute. Thus, a voyage which had started out with six pages of puffery in the New York *Journal of Commerce,* ended up making daily headlines in The *New York Times.* Finally, the Venezuelan dock workers agreed to unload the ship, but by hand,

and provided she didn't come back—at least not until some kind of a special compensatory arrangement could be worked out. She then languished in Baltimore for two years, and never did succeed in her much-heralded South American mission.

Finally Charlie could discern the ungainly profile of his ship. Blacked-out and riding at anchor, she had not one gunboat around her now. She looked huge. The giant boxes stacked on her deck swelled her silhouette. But they gave her the square lines of a building instead of a boat. Coming closer, he could see the white superstructure and the white smokestack, ghostly pale against the moonless sky. "She's dead all right," he thought. "Even if we come back at six or seven in the morning, it'll take four hours to get the plant going and bring her back to life." As their fishing boat slid alongside the high back hull, Charlie could hear Cambodian voices coming from the bridge.

"The guards are still aboard, Cliff," he said. "I wonder what they took?"

Harrington had decided on the way out from Koh Tang, there was one good thing about coming back to the ship. He could pick up his wallet. Not that there was much in it: fourteen dollars, his seaman's papers, and his driver's license. But it contained his social security card—the original card from when he was a boy and had worked part time on a tugboat named the *Slocum* in San Francisco Bay. The edges were chewed and there was a six-cent airmail stamp stuck to the back. Hell, he could get a new one anytime. And who in Christ's name needs social security in Cambodia, he suddenly thought. Still, he wanted the card.

He was climbing up the pilot's ladder thinking about his social security card when the first bomb burst. At least the instant he heard the explosion and saw the blinding flash of light, he thought it was a bomb. Seven or eight of the Cambodians and the captain had already gone up the ladder and were standing on the deck. In the bomb's glare he could see the Cambodians run for cover. Then there was another burst and another, an earsplitting chain of explosions. He looked up and saw an orange glow sailing out of the sky, which suddenly detonated in a brilliant flash of white light. These aren't bombs, yet they're not flares either, he realized. They're some kind of giant flashbulbs for taking aerial photographs that burst in the sky. On the next pass, Harrington heard the plane coming before it sowed the sky with its light-giving missiles. He also heard the panic-stricken Cambodians shouting for him and the captain to abandon ship.

"The shit's really running down their backs," said Charlie. "Anyway, they seem to have lost interest in looking in the rooms." As the fishing boat plodded back towards Koh Tang, Charlie kept his eyes on the *Mayaguez,* getting smaller and smaller off the stern. He could still see the flashes of light bursting above her, as his ship continued to have her picture taken.

Perhaps it was fatigue finally settling in, or maybe it was a captain's inbred desire to stay with his ship, but he didn't want to go back to the island. Or to his crew. Friedler, what did he say? "Now what's the old man gettin' us into." And Myregard. Maybe he's right. "They're just trying to pacify us, Captain." That's what Myregard said. Myregard doesn't believe they're going to bring us back to the ship in the morning. He thinks they're going to chop our heads off.

He had never really believed the Cambodians would do that. Ann's probably scared to death they will, he thought. He knew how nervous his wife was. If the TV fellas show up to interview her, she'll probably lock the door and run out of the house, he thought. The vision of that happening made him smile. Anyway, she's got a good insurance policy on me. And she can always go live with one of her brothers. The one with the supermarket chain in Joliet, probably. Well, Annie and me, we've had some great times together, he thought. And as the fishing boat throbbed back towards the harbor, Charlie Miller remembered the days when he was courting Ann Polerasky aboard the cruise ship *Leilani*.

He had worked his way up from third mate to staff captain. She was the trained nurse in charge of the children. They sailed together for a year before they finally got married on a Thanksgiving cruise to Acapulco in 1957. A Benedictine monk married them in the little church in the town square. But it was against company policy for husband and wife to work on the same ship. In those days they didn't even let two brothers or a father and son work on the same ship. So he and Annie had to keep their marriage a secret. Charlie, of course, had to go on doing all the things the staff captain was expected to do: dancing with all the single women at night and buying everybody drinks. "But I made it a ship's rule," Charlie said, "that no officer could escort a woman passenger to her stateroom without having another officer present. Otherwise, some of those women would tear off their clothes and holler rape." Charlie always thought the priests were the nicest passengers. It was usually the priests he would buy the drinks for. "They were the people who treated me best on any ship I was on," Charlie used to explain. "I used to say, 'hey, Dad, let's go get a shot.' I never called them 'Father.' But having a wife aboard got to be a strain. I used to have to sneak Annie up to my cabin just to eat dinner."

The fishing boat reentered the crescent-shaped harbor and slid silently alongside the other fishing boat with the rest of the *Mayaguez* crew. Charlie could see the men sprawled out on the deck trying to sleep. Overhead he could hear the American plane keeping its all-night vigil. He glanced at the luminous dial on his watch: 12:15. Six hours before they would go back to the ship.

Commander Jim Messegee glanced up at the battery of clocks on the OPCON room wall: 1715 Zulu time, 0115 Hotel time in Subic, and 1315 Romeo time in the Pentagon. He was coming up on thirty hours in the OPCON room, though the flow of coffee from the electric urn over on the counter and the flow of adrenalin in his own body, had kept him feeling pretty chipper. Nevertheless, he had decided to go downstairs and sack out for a couple of hours. Brandt was there to take over.

Commander William Brandt Powell was not only Jim Messegee's exec, he was his best friend. The Philippine Air Patrol Group at Cubi Point was the fourth place they had served together. Even Brandt's wife, Susan, and his wife, Marlene, had become buddies.

Messegee stepped into the radio shack adjoining the OPCON room and made a final check. Nothing new. Not much had happened since they dropped the flares about two hours ago. They had spotted a boat with some people on it going back to the *Mayaguez*. At first, they suspected the Cambodians might be bringing back the crew to move the ship. But under the brilliant barrage of flares, they had observed the tiny figures below crawling back off the ship onto the fishing boat. Then they had watched the boat return to Koh Tang. President Ford, Messegee knew, had issued orders that the Cambodians were not to move the American ship. The TAC Birds would stop them if they did.

Messegee went downstairs and stretched out on the couch in his office. It had been an exciting day, the kind that made him wish he'd never been promoted to commander. "I want to be in one of those birds so bad I can taste it," he had said to Brandt Powell at least a dozen times during the past thirty hours. "We've got to sit around the goddamn OPCON room while all the fun's going on."

This morning at first light, at about 2300 *Z,* he had ordered one of his P3 Orions to get down and eyeball the *Mayaguez* up close. The electronic sensor operators had been observing the ship all night. But Messegee thought there might be more than one ship around. A few days earlier, he knew that the Cambodians had stopped some other ships. He wanted to make sure his birds had the right ship. "Go down and read the name off the bow," he instructed the pilot. The plane went down and took a hit in the tail. "How close did you get?" Messegee queried the pilot.

"Within a thousand yards, Skipper," the pilot's voice came back over the radio.

"What do you mean, within a thousand yards?" asked Messegee.

"Well within a thousand yards, Skipper. Close enough to tell they had about forty rifles and machine guns shootin' at us."

This afternoon another P3 Orion had observed two fishing boats take some of the crew from the *Mayaguez* to Koh Tang. They couldn't tell how many men were on the boats. But some of the crew at least, they were sure had been transferred to the island. Then it had gotten dark. They couldn't tell if the men were still on the fishing boats or somewhere on the beach. One thing was sure. The Cambodians had pretty good anti-aircraft on the island. The cockpit observers could see the tracer rounds come up from Koh Tang and then arc over and fall.

Jim Messegee finally dropped off to sleep.

NINE

Night Murmurs off Koh Tang

SECOND MATE JERRY MYREGARD had used the last gleamings of daylight to size up Koh Tang. His eyes had swept the island seeking things he would need: flotation, food, liquid, as well as dense tropical foliage to keep himself concealed. Twenty-four hours earlier, under Dave English's goading, he had thought more in terms of assault—grabbing the Cambodians' guns and throwing the little men overboard. Now his mind was on escape. Far simpler. He didn't have to convince anyone. Coombes, Harrington, Newman, and the captain as well, they were all older, meeker, and who knows, maybe wiser men too. But he remembered the chief mate's face. Looked at me like I was crazy for even mentioning that one alternative might be to grab the Cambodians, slip the anchor, and run. And Harrington, what did he say? "Pull a stunt like that and somebody's going to get killed." Only English got the picture. But maybe he was too gung ho. The big ex-Marine was ready to kill everybody. Anyway, Myregard thought, it probably wouldn't work. Too many Cambodians. But one good man with a little nerve, strength, and endurance could melt into the night and escape.

"Anyway," said Jerry Myregard to himself, "you always were a loner."

He had already started to prepare. This morning on his watch, he had pored over the chart, memorizing the reefs, rocks, and sub-atolls like Koh Pring a few miles west. This afternoon he had debated doing his exercises, but had finally done them. Now he regretted it. Should have saved every ounce of strength. Tonight, before darkness blotted out the beach and jungle behind it, he had studied the island. A couple of skiffs rested on the beach, but no paddles. It didn't matter. He had already decided to cross over the hill to the other side of the island. "Put as much distance as you can between yourself and your captors," he had told himself. Over there, well, first he'd hide. He'd need coconuts. The milk would keep him from dehydrating. Then he'd look for a skiff, a board or a tree trunk, so he could float away from Koh Tang. To where? Well, first to Koh Pring. Then to a passing ship, a Thai fishing boat, or the Thai border.

Sitting on the deck of the Cambodian fishing boat, Myregard peered off into the darkness. There was no moon. He could barely see the strip of white separating sea and jungle. The hill behind had been swallowed up by the night.

"All right, Myregard," he said, "here's your chance." He glanced around the deck. The other crew members were curled up on fish nets, sprawled over the hatches, or propped against the wooden rail trying to sleep. Their Cambodian guards were dozing too. But it was his own shipmates who worried him. What if somebody saw him go and yelled: "man overboard!"

He began taking quick, short breaths, pumping oxygen into his blood. The night air tasted cool and moist. Overhead he could hear the undulating drone of the recon plane. The "grinder" English had named it. The screeching jets had gone. But the steady drone which had replaced them, tantalized the shore gunners even more. Every now and then they'd cut loose, spraying streams of orange tracers up towards the sound. Once he saw the plane's landing lights snap on. That pilot's trying to bait them, he thought, rubbing it in that he's up there circling at an unreachable altitude for their small-calibre anti-aircraft guns.

"All right, Myregard," he repeated to himself. "You're in great physical condition. You've been training for years. Now, hyperventilate and slip over the side. Nobody'll see you go."

But he didn't go and it made him mad. "Scared?" he asked himself. No, not scared. But earlier this evening the Cambodian who spoke French, the one talking to Pantryman Pastrano, had said they would be going back to the ship at six o'clock in the morning. "Tomorrow," Myregard said. "If they don't take us back to the ship, I'll go tomorrow."

Burt Coombes hoped he could drift off for a few hours at least, but the rolled-up fish net he was lying on just wasn't conducive to sleep. The net's rough twine cut into his back. Besides, it stank of dead fish.

Lying there on the deck of the Cambodian fishing boat gazing out at the dark outline of the island, Coombes contemplated the advice that an old captain, John Avery, had given him some years ago when he was third mate on the *Hong Kong Bear*. Avery had been a Whangpoo river pilot in Shanghai, and immediately following Pearl Harbor, had been incarcerated by the Japs. "They were cruel captors," he told Coombes. "It's a known fact," added Avery, "most Orientals treat their prisoners like animals." "Escape if you can," he urged his third mate, if by any chance he ever had the misfortune to be captured in Asia. "And if you can't escape, show your rank. Orientals appreciate rank." He then told Coombes about how as the prison camp leader he had traded his cigarette ration to a guard, who in exchange sharpened Avery's razor every morning. That way Avery could keep up appearances. "Very important," he advised.

Coombes glanced at the human forms sprawled over the deck. To the Cambodians, he thought, we must all look alike. How could they tell rank? Well, at least they knew who was captain. "I'll just stick with the skipper," he said to himself.

Coombes had heard some dangerous talk back aboard the *Mayaguez*. What did English say? "If I can grab one of those grenade-launchers, Burt, you'll see these gooks goin' overboard."

Captain Charles T. Miller, on the port wing of the bridge. ROY RO-
WAN PHOTO

The *Mayaguez.*

Burton B. Coombes, third mate on the twelve-to-four watch, taking bearing with the azimuth circle on the starboard wing of the bridge, as he was doing when he spotted the gunboat. ROY ROWAN PHOTO

Juan P. Sanchez, second assistant engineer, who heard the Voice of America broadcast about *Mayaguez* on Tuesday, May 13. ROY RO-WAN PHOTO

Left: James P. Newman, chief mate. *Below left:* Clifford J. Harrington, chief engineer. *Below right:* Vernon P. Greenlin, first engineer. ROY ROWAN PHOTOS

Above left: David C. English, third mate on the eight-to-twelve watch. A former Marine, he led the group that considered overpowering the Cambodians. *Above right:* Tyrone Matthews, wiper, had been aboard another cargo ship that had hit by an amor-piercing shell. He was a paratrooper in Vietnam. *Below left:* Ordinary Seaman Anastacio C. Sereno, who was at the helm when the ship was fired on. *Below right:* Americo Faria, oiler. He was on deck when the gunboat fired rockets across the bow. He thought the ship had been hit. ROY ROWAN PHOTOS

Above left: Able-Bodied Seaman Gerald Bayless. *Above right:* Ordinary Seaman Gerardo Lopez. *Below left:* Messman Munasser T. Omer. *Below right:* Messman Kassem Saleh. ROY ROWAN PHOTOS

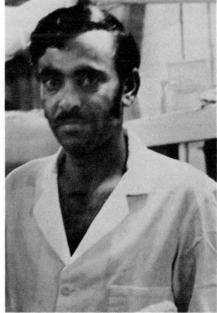

Air Force General David Jones, acting chairman of the Joint Chiefs of Staff, makes a key point during a National Security Council meeting. Listening are *(from left)* Robert S. Ingersoll, assistant secretary of state; President Ford; Defense Secretary James Schlesinger; William P. Clements, Jr., deputy secretary of defense; Presidential Counselor Jack Marsh; Secretary of State Henry A. Kissinger; Vice-President Rockefeller; and CIA Director William E. Colby. OFFICIAL WHITE HOUSE PHOTO BY DAVID HUME KENNERLY

Destroyed and damaged helicopters on Koh Tang. AIR FORCE PHOTO

Left: Commander James A. Messegee, Philippine Air Patrol Group, in his office at Cubi Point, Subic Bay. *Below left:* Commander J. Michael Rodgers, captain of U.S.S. *Henry B. Wilson. Below right:* Commander Robert A. Peterson, captain of U.S.S. *Harold E. Holt.* ROY ROWAN PHOTOS

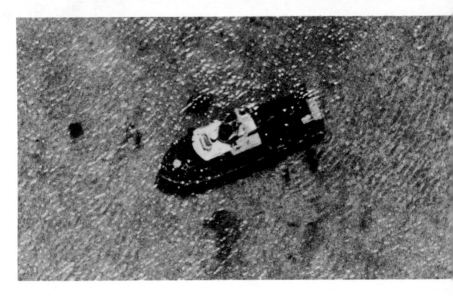

Sunken patrol boat 800 meters east of Koh Tang. AIR FORCE PHOTO

U.S. Marines run from a CH-53 helicopter during rescue operations of the merchant vessel *Mayaguez.* Koh Tang, Cambodia. AIR FORCE PHOTO

The U.S.S. *Wilson* continues its suppressive barrage while the *Mayaguez* is being rescued, Koh Tang. AIR FORCE PHOTO

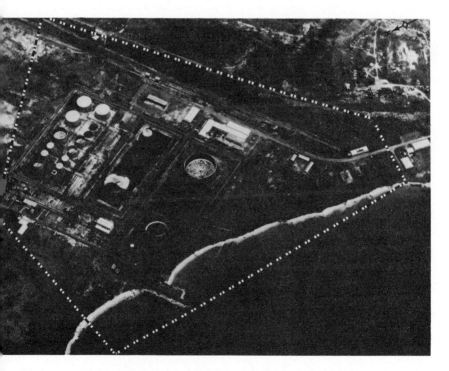

Kompong Som Pol Refinery. AIR FORCE PHOTO

U.S. Marines board the *Mayaguez* from the U.S.S. *Harold E. Holt.* DEPT. OF DEFENSE PHOTO

Thai fishing boat bringing freed *Mayaguez* crewman to U.S.S. *Henry B. Wilson.* COPYRIGHT © 1975 BY WAYNE STEWART

Crewmen of the U.S.S. *Henry B. Wilson* assist *Mayaguez* crewmen aboard the destroyer. COPYRIGHT © 1975 BY WAYNE STEWART

Mayaguez crewmen aboard destroyer U.S.S. *Henry B. Wilson*. COPYRIGHT © 1975 BY WAYNE STEWART

The U.S.S. *Holt* towing the *Mayaguez*. AIR FORCE PHOTO

The author interviewing President Ford. OFFICIAL WHITE HOUSE
PHOTO BY DAVID HUME KENNERLY

And Friedler, he was right there with English. "Might as well try," he said. "We're going to get killed, anyway, when they take us ashore."

"These Cambodian kids look a little nervous to me," Coombes had protested. "I'd rather go to prison camp than be a dead hero."

Coombes tilted his face up at the black, star-filled sky and listened to the reconnaissance plane flying round and round over Koh Tang. He couldn't see it, but the sound was reassuring. At least they know we're down here, he thought. Have they told Delores yet? he wondered. He had just spent five months on the beach, "playing golf, fishing, and fighting with my wife," as he had said to his new shipmates on the *Mayaguez*. But Burt appreciated how tough a sailor's life was on a wife. "You come home and upset the applecart," he said. "Your old lady is used to being on her own." Delores, he suddenly thought, might be on her own for a long time.

Burt and Delores had fallen in love on a blind date in San Francisco. Burt's brother Jim had fallen in love with Delores too. Only Jim shipped out to New Guinea and Burt and Delores got married. They had one daughter, Linda, a real knockout whom Burt missed seeing crowned homecoming queen of Richmond High, because as usual, he was away at sea. It had been Delores and Linda together who finally made Burt join Gamblers Anonymous, even though on ships he was a winner. On the *Mohawk* he won so much money playing poker they called him the "Iron Fist." But on shore he was a big loser. "I'll bet on anything," he always said, "football, basketball, horses, dice, cards, lotteries, stocks, you name it." One night he dropped $3,000 shooting dice in Las Vegas and wired Delores for bus money home. "Walk!" she wired back.

Quite surprisingly, especially to him, it was the members of Gamblers Anonymous who had become his best friends. They were the people he missed most sailing around the Orient. From Saigon last month he had written a letter to one of his friends back home in GA: "Well, here I am gambling my ass on the Vietnam war."

Coming in to Koh Tang on the Cambodian fishing boat, Cliff Harrington had apologized for having made a bet with him. Harrington, Coombes, and English had each put up five dollars on the Masters. Harrington picked Nicklaus, Coombes picked Weiskopf, and English picked Johnny Miller. Nicklaus won and Weiskopf and Miller tied for runner-up. "I'm going to give you that five bucks back," Harrington said on the fishing boat. "You shouldn't have bet. And it's brought me nothing but bad luck."

We'll just have to see if it's brought me bad luck too, Burt Coombes thought.

Second Engineer Juan Sanchez couldn't sleep, although A-rab Sam, the crew messman, complained that he was snoring so loud he was keeping everybody else on the Cambodian fishing boat awake. Sam, as Kassem Saleh was also called, and Sanchez had been shipmates twice before. In fact, on the *San Francisco* they had worked together in the Black Gang, Sam having formerly been a wiper. "You're making more noise than the machine guns," said Sam.

Actually, Sanchez had been lying on his back watching the tracers crisscross the sky, thinking about how he was going to start up the plant in the morning. The captain had told him that they would start back for the *Mayaguez* at six, right in the middle of his four-to-eight watch. So Sanchez was making mental notes of all the things he'd have to do. The emergency generator would kick out, he knew, unless you put a pretty good load on it. And there would be barely enough electricity to run the blower and fuel-oil pump to bring steam out. You had to use a lot of little tricks to start up an old plant like that. Actually, Sanchez had expected to be there, sort of looking after the machinery all the time. He hadn't confided this to anybody, but right up until the last minute when the Cambodians came down and forced everybody out of the engineroom at gunpoint, he had been planning to hide and stay aboard ship. "With all the canned food and water on this ship," he had told himself, "I can live for months."

Sparks had come down there, too, trying to hide. "What are they going to do to us?" he had kept asking Sanchez.

"Don't worry, we're going to be free," Sanchez had said, trying to calm the radio operator. He sat the radio operator down under the blower in the machine shop, and then went down to the transfer pump at the bottom of the lower flat to hide. When he looked back up, he saw all the black pajama pants. He could only see legs. But soon he saw the chief's legs, and the first's legs, and Faria the oiler's legs, and Conway the fireman's legs, and they were all going up the ladder, leaving.

"Well," Sanchez had said to himself, "the only one left is me." But he suddenly thought, what if the Cambodians mine the ship and blow it up. I'd be dead. So Sanchez came up on deck and one of the Cambodians pointed his gun at him, and he climbed down into the fishing boat on the port side with the chief.

Bedded down on the deck of the fishing boat as a Black Gang threesome, were Wiper Matthews, Fireman Guerrero, and Oiler Faria. Faria was mad at himself for forgetting to bring his "79" pipe tobacco. And now as he stared up at the sky, straining to glimpse the reconnaissance plane which he could hear buzzing over them like a mosquito, he had nothing to smoke. Guerrero was not mad, but worried. He had left a thousand dollars in cash in an envelope in his locker. When Faria hurriedly left their cabin to get on the fishing boat, he had forgotten to lock the door. Tyrone Matthews, the ex–Special Forces paratrooper from Vietnam, was sleeping blissfully, having tuned out the angry tattoo of machine guns coming from the island. He awoke refreshed. "A lot of stars were out. It was cool. And I slept beautiful," he said to Guerrero.

In the long interval since World War II, Faria had forgotten how to tune out machine guns and go to sleep. The chatter of fifty-calibre coming from Koh Tang reminded him of a night during the invasion of Luzon in 1945. Faria's infantry company had just landed and his squad had been ordered out on night patrol. "Let me sleep, I'm tired," Faria had pleaded. His good buddy, who amazed everybody by the way he would keep on shooting like Audie Murphy no matter how many Japs there were, went instead. But that night there were too many Japs. His buddy didn't come back. Faria found him with bullet holes in his head and body, though he hardly recognized him because he'd turned brown in the sun. Faria rolled his buddy down the hill. Now as the machine guns over on the shore at Koh Tang kept him from sleep, he tried to think of his buddy's name. But he couldn't. He had always thought of him as Audie.

Gerardo Lopez and Gerald Bayless were cabin-mates on the *Mayaguez* and they stuck together that night on the fishing boat as well. When the boat had first arrived at Koh Tang, Bayless had taken off his shoes and socks and rolled up his pants to wade ashore. But over on the shore, he saw one of the Cambodian gunners waving the boat off. He wasn't sure why. Maybe, Bayless thought, he doesn't want us too close to his anti-aircraft gun position. Or perhaps the Cambodian feared that if those Americans came ashore, some of them might melt away into the jungle. In any case, their fishing boat had backed off the beach and anchored. Soon Bayless picked up a rumor. Electrician Wilfredo Reyes, a pretty fair linguist, had somehow managed a conversation with one of the Cambodian guards. "They're going to take us to another place farther down the island," Reyes had told Bayless. "They've got a big prison camp down there." Lying on the deck of the fishing boat, Bayless still figured that's where they were going.

Gerardo Lopez didn't understand the Cambodians at Koh Tang. They weren't friendly like the Cambodians he had met when he was on the *Steel Traveller* and they had been rocketed in that Cambodian port, the name of which he couldn't remember. One of the Cambodian guards at that port had given him a set of rare postcards showing a Cambodian water buffalo sacrifice ceremony.

The guard had said: "We don't print postcards like this in Cambodia anymore. Please, you take them back to America and keep them."

Dave English had spread his 250 pounds of flesh over the same fish net with Burt Coombes and was trying to sleep. He never closed his eyes. He still had on his khaki shorts and T-shirt. The jeans and long-sleeved shirt which he had laid out to wear ashore were back in his cabin. The Cambodians hadn't given him a chance to change. But as he understood it from Pantryman Pastrano's Cajun French conversation with the quartermaster of one of the gunboats, they were going back to the *Mayaguez* early in the morning. But he wasn't sure. "We got a piss-poor language relationship," he said to himself.

Ten thousand feet above he could hear the grinder going around and around like a cement mixer in the sky. Every time the grinder got directly overhead, the shore batteries would cut loose, spraying orange tracers into the blackness above their fishing boat. The Cambodians, he decided from the sound, had bigger stuff than fifty-calibre over on the beach: a Chinese thirty-seven–millimeter cannon, he thought. English considered himself something of a ballistics expert. At Camp Barstow he had been on the pistol and rifle team.

"So here we are," Dave English said to Burt Coombes. "All screwed up like fire and boat drill." Coombes had mentioned how much he'd like to have a hamburger with some french fries and a nice cold glass of beer. English didn't worry about that stuff. He was thinking, instead, how he wished he'd filled out an allotment form for Cora. They lived in Manila. She didn't need an allotment because on the *Mayaguez* he got into Manila often enough and could give Cora the money himself. "Now what's she going to do?" he asked himself.

English had first met Cora in Legaspie City. He was on the *Creighton Victory,* and had run into Cora's father, an exporter of

Philippine mahogany logs. The old man brought bachelor English home to meet his five daughters. Now they had two daughters of their own, Genevieve and Apple. "If I ever get out of here," he vowed, "I'll move them to Seattle." But to get out of there, Dave English expected they might have to kill some Cambodians. There were more Cambodians now—eighty or ninety he guessed on the fishing boats and gunboats assembled in the harbor at Koh Tang. He had no idea how many more armed men there might be ashore. English had been keeping careful track of the gunboats, anyway. So far he had noted four different gunboats close enough to read the numbers: 128, 126, 125, and 130. One of them, number 126, flew the Viet Cong flag. Not just some homemade pennant, flown perhaps to celebrate the Viet Cong victory in Saigon, but a regular factory-made flag. He wondered if the capture of the *Mayaguez* could have been a joint venture.

Cliff Harrington had been trying to get to sleep ever since he and Charlie had come back from their aborted trip to the *Mayaguez.* Now, lying on his back on the deck of the fishing boat, he looked up at the stars and listened to the drone of the night watchman the U.S. government had stationed there. For some reason, he was thinking of his dead brother, William Francis Harrington. Climbing up to the deck of the *Mayaguez,* three hours earlier, with the blinding illumination bombs bursting above, he had suddenly thought of Bill. He wondered if it might have looked like that the night the Germans shot Bill's B-17 out of the sky.

Charlie Miller had been trying to sleep on the same cramped hatch cover with the chief. For some reason he had got to thinking about his brother, Oliver James Miller. Ollie had been dead for a long time. But three hours earlier standing on the deck of the *Mayaguez* with the brilliant, acrid flares exploding all around his ship, Charlie wondered if it might have looked like that the night the Germans blew up the old *Oregonian* on its way to Murmansk with a load of ammunition and Oliver aboard.

Charlie looked up at the stars and listened to the reassuring sound of the reconnaissance plane circling overhead. Then he drifted off to sleep.

Wednesday, May 14

TEN

Rocket Attack

WHEN CHARLIE MILLER awoke from a brief, fitful sleep he found half a dozen Cambodian guards curled up with their guns on the same hatch cover with him and the chief. The rest of his crew lay sprawled over the decks of the two fishing boats. He gazed over at the beach. It was quiet now. The shore gunners had given up on the reconnaissance plane which had droned through the night. Behind the beach the dark contour of Koh Tang's lone hill loomed up against the purple light of morning.

He felt terrible. His back ached and his mouth tasted chalky. In fact, he felt about as bad as those mornings years ago after he had played Sparky Taylor's game. Sparky had been captain of a Yangtze River transit boat in western China until he got hit in the chest with a meat cleaver during a pirate attack. But aboard the *President Taft,* which Sparky signed on as an AB after his wound had healed, he introduced Charlie to his game. Sparky would put a bottle of whiskey, a case of beer, and a can of paint on the table and challenge all comers to a duel—which often as not, turned out to be Charlie. Sparky and Charlie would then take turns slugging down the whiskey and chug-a-lugging the beer until one of them passed out, and the other got to paint his face.

Charlie studied his watch. It was difficult to make out—too light for the luminous dial to shine, too dark to read. Twenty-five past five, he thought. Suddenly he remembered Myregard's warning: "I may not be around in the morning, Skipper." Pretty level-headed mate, Jerry. But last night Myregard admitted he was ready to make a break for it. "We're all too complacent, Captain," he said. "I'm not going to sit around here and wait for them to chop off our heads."

Myregard had upset Charlie. He needed his second mate. Besides, he worried what the Cambodians would do if one of the crew turned out to be missing. "Pull something like that, and we all may get our heads chopped off," Charlie said.

Charlie's eyes swept over the decks of the two fishing boats seeking Myregard's blonde head. He's gone, Charlie thought. Then he spotted the second mate sitting propped up against an oil drum on the other boat. Myregard was awake, his head turning and surveying the sleeping guards. Too late now, Charlie thought. In another ten minutes it'll be light.

At six o'clock, the hour the Cambodians had told Charlie they would take them back to the *Mayaguez,* the two fishing boats were still lashed together fifty yards off Koh Tang's white sand beach. He could see three gunboats in the harbor now. They bobbed at anchor as the sky started to glow pink, showing signs of a spectacular sunrise. Charlie watched the sun come. For an instant, only the upper rim showed, a crescent of fire at the top of the hill. Then the whole sky burst into flame. In thirty minutes he knew the day would be burning hot.

"How about it, Charlie?" said Harrington, who was now sitting up and rubbing his eyes. "We gonna get hotel money for last night? Union rule. We're in port and we couldn't sleep aboard."

At eight o'clock the Cambodian guards herded everybody into the bigger of the two fishing boats and headed out of the harbor. The fishing boat had already struck Charlie as a peculiar looking craft, at least by American standards. All the weight was in the stern—the pilot house, bunkhouse, engineroom, and galley, having been built into the fantail. Now, even with the forty-man crew of the *Mayaguez* crowded on the forward deck, he noticed that she still rode way down in the ass. The Cambodian guards were scattered over the boat: two in the bow, four or five inside the pilot house, and a couple tucked under the overhang back in the stern. There was plenty of unoccupied space atop the pilot house, but the guards wouldn't let any of the *Mayaguez* crew climb up.

Even as they had started out of the harbor, Charlie felt uncertainty. So far this morning he had had no communication with his captors. The Cambodian ensign was not aboard. The guard with the U.S. Army fieldpack radio was buried away in the pilot house. The only officialdom Charlie could see were the two armed guards with AK-47s standing in the bow. Their faces were noncommittal. All he had to go on was last night's promise, from the man who called himself the driver, that they would be taken back to the *Mayaguez* at six o'clock in the morning. It was now after eight, but at this moment the bow of the fishing boat was pointed at a black speck in the distance, which Charlie knew to be the *Mayaguez*. Two gunboats ranged out ahead, zipping over the shimmering azure sea.

It's going to take three or four hours to get the plant going, he thought. Then we'll see what these fellows want to do. Who knows, maybe they'll let us go.

The fishing boat steered steadily for the *Mayaguez*. Charlie began to feel better. The sun's rays were baking the ache out of his back. He felt alert. Eighteen hours of fasting, even though it had not been voluntary, had cleared his mind. Things are definitely looking up, he decided. Then suddenly the fishing boat veered to starboard. For an instant Charlie thought the helmsman might have let go the wheel to light a cigarette. But the boat kept to its new course, heading northeast.

"They're just giving us a line of bullshit," he heard his big red-headed third mate, Dave English, bellow.

English had made it a point to position himself in the bow next to the two armed Cambodians. Perhaps it was his negative outlook working on him again. Or maybe it was just the way the two gunboats went skipping off ahead, running scared, headed for the mainland, he had decided. But English had been nursing an uneasy feeling all morning that they weren't going back to their ship.

"It's just a big pile of bullshit," he repeated, glaring into the blank faces of the two Cambodians. He felt like grabbing one of their AK-47s and spraying the little white pilot house with bullets. "Hey, Skipper," he said, "looks like we're headed for Kompong Som."

The screech of six jets drowned English out. Streaking by in pairs they flashed over the fishing boat, a rapid succession of sonic booms exploding in everybody's ears. The planes darted off across the water. Seconds later English could see them climbing and diving out on the horizon in a graceful aerial ballet. The muted sound of distant rockets and bombs drifted back to the fishing boat. They're trying to turn the two gunboats around, English decided. Then, half-confirming this thought, he saw the two tiny grey specks that were the gunboats, split. One turned back for Koh Tang. The other still raced on for the mainland and Kompong Som. English saw the planes continue diving and climbing. But he didn't believe they were really trying to hit the one that had not turned around. Then his sharp eyes picked out a black puff of smoke, no bigger than an exclamation mark, hanging over the horizon. You can drop a bomb in the sea, English knew, but you won't raise black smoke like that unless you hit something. For some reason he didn't mention what he had seen to the captain, who was standing next to him. He wasn't sure what change in American tactics the bombing of the gunboat might signify. It could mean their fishing boat would be next.

English glanced down at his wrist, forgetting that his watch was back on the *Mayaguez*.

"What time is it, Captain?" he asked.

"Eight-thirty," answered Charlie. "Exactly eight-thirty." English was sure Charlie Miller hadn't seen the puff of smoke.

There wasn't much time for English to try and figure out what sudden change in American tactics the puff of black smoke might signify. He looked up. The jets had wheeled and were now streaking straight at the fishing boat.

"Here they come," he yelled. The first two planes swept by high on the port side, banked, and dove on the fishing boat from behind. Twin geysers erupted from the sea 100 feet off the bow.

"They're going to kill us all!" English heard a voice cry out.

The second pair of jets streaked in from the stern, and two more geysers erupted off the bow, coming even closer to the fishing boat.

"Rockets!" hollered English. "They're firing rockets!"

He saw the two Cambodians crouch down against the gunwhale, as if the wooden bow rail could shield them against the high explosives raining down. If one of those babies hits this boat, it'll blow it to splinters, he thought. He knew the planes hadn't tried to hit them so far. Those flyboys are better shots than that. But how long would they wait? That puff of black smoke could only mean one thing. The pilots now had orders to shoot to kill!

What the planes had been doing out on the horizon, they were now doing directly above the fishing boat—banking, diving, swooping, and soaring back up into the sky. Each time they dove, two more plumes of water shot up in front of the fishing boat. English looked up and waved. Maybe, he thought, the pilots would be able to see him. Maybe if they know it's us they won't blow the boat up.

The fishing boat kept to its course and the pilots accepted the challenge. They swooped in closer. Now the geysers erupted fifty feet from the bow. Jesus Christ, English thought, they're going to do it. He saw the men clustered next to the gasoline drums in front of the pilot house instinctively move away. But there was no place to hide.

The next pair of jets altered the flight pattern. Instead of pouncing on the fishing boat from behind, they streaked by first port-to-starboard, then starboard-to-port. This time a quick succession of shell-bursts exploded in English's ear. He knew that sound well.

Twenty-millimeter cannons, every fourth shell with a high explosive head. He could tell from the curtain of water rising on the two sides of the fishing boat.

"Jesus Christ, they're coming close," he yelled, as a piece of shrapnel dropped like a fiery hot hailstone down the back of his shirt. English rolled over on the deck trying to shake the shrapnel out, when his hand hit another searing piece. It was smaller than a nickel, but he could feel the flesh sizzle. He glanced over and saw blood streaming from the second mate's right arm. Myregard was crouched against the gunwhale and didn't seem to notice.

"You OK?" English asked.

Myregard looked down and saw the blood. He felt no pain, only fury at himself for not having done what he had planned to do last night. "Stupid sonofabitch," he said to himself. "You should have gone over the side."

English grabbed Myregard's arm and started squeezing. He wanted to try and get the sulphurous piece of steel out of the second mate's arm before it began to fester. He didn't have a knife to cut the flesh with, so he kept on squeezing. But the jagged steel fragment was too deeply imbedded. Finally, English tied up the wound with a handkerchief.

"I think those pilots are trying to tell us something, Jerry," he said. "They're hoping we'll grab this boat away from the Cambodians." Myregard, he could see, was seething inside.

English glanced up at the bow. The two Cambodian guards had dived into the fish well to get away from the flying shrapnel. Their two AK-47s were lying on the deck for anyone to pick up. "I'll be goddamned if I want to go like a lamb to the slaughter," English said, inching towards the two guns. His eyes suddenly met the captain's, who had spotted the guns, too. And for the first time since they had been captured, English thought the old man was actually egging him on. "Pick up those two rifles, English," his eyes seemed to be saying. Just then the hatch cover lifted up and the two chagrined Cambodians climbed out of the fish well. "They'll be back in there before this party's over," English said to himself.

Myregard, he noticed, had started to move towards the stern. "Hey, Jerry, check what's going on inside the pilot house," he shouted after the second mate. "Maybe we can grab this boat yet. Talk to the guys back there. See who's ready to go." The second mate nodded. English watched him walk aft with the handkerchief knotted around his arm.

When he turned, English saw Bayless gesturing to Sereno and LaBue. He could hear Bayless starting to sound off, before the next sortie drowned him out. "They want to grab those fucking guns," he heard Bayless say. "It's all talk. A lot of fucking bullshit. But we better stop 'em before they get us shot."

Sereno was one sailor English felt he could count on. He was big and strong and level-headed. But Sereno wasn't thinking of staging any shipboard revolt. He was praying. God, he knew, wouldn't let him down. And when he saw all the jets, he knew President Ford wouldn't let him down, either. But he feared the flying steel fragments. As a thirteen-year-old in Manila, it was a chunk of Japanese shrapnel which had torn out his left eye.

Next to Sereno, two other Filipinos: Wilfredo Reyes, the twenty-six-year-old electrician, and his father Guillermo Reyes, the fifty-three-year-old cook, were praying too. Reyes senior had been a Philippine scout during World War II, but at this moment he was frightened as he had never been in the war. His eyes were lowered in prayer when they seized on the crimson blot spreading down the right leg of Al Rappenecker's white coveralls.

Third Engineer Rappenecker had been crouched down in the small fish hatch at midships. At first he decided the hatch was a good place to be, since it offered a little protection against the flying steel fragments. But then he looked down and saw the gas drums below and decided, if they ever hit those, the whole hatch with him on it would be blown to smithereens. He had just stood up to move when a cluster of shell fragments caught him in the leg.

Rappenecker hardly felt them hit. But when he looked down

and saw the blood spreading like the Red Sea over his white
coveralls, he thought, I'll do what they do in the cowboy books and
stick plugs in the holes. Fortunately, Charlie Miller also saw the
blood gushing from the third engineer's coveralls. He came over
and made a tourniquet out of his handkerchief and tied it around
Rappenecker's leg. Charlie had determined right at the beginning
of the attack that the pilots were only trying to turn the fishing boat
around. But now they were coming too close. He had never seen
such shooting. The pilots were laying down their fire closer than
the Japs had when he was aboard the *Stanford Newell* in Leyte
Gulf. And the Japs had been trying to hit his ship, not miss it.

Charlie had just finished binding up Rappenecker's wounds
when he saw pieces of flying steel rip through the front of the pilot
house. He couldn't see if the helmsman had been hit. The boat
swerved to port, and Charlie saw one of the Cambodian guards
jump up and point his AK-47 in the pilot house door. The helmsman hadn't been hit. He was merely trying to turn the boat away
from the fire. Strange, Charlie thought. Why does he have to point
a gun at his own helmsman?

Charlie didn't have time to worry about the helmsman. He
looked up and saw Juan Sanchez with his hand cupped around his
left ear, blood dripping through his fingers. Just a few days earlier
Sanchez had come up to Charlie and said: "Hey, Cap, you don't
remember me, do you? I was a fireman on the *General Gordon*
when you were the chief mate." Sanchez was right. He didn't
remember him at all. He reached for his handkerchief to mop the
second engineer's ear, when he suddenly remembered that he had
already tied it around the third engineer's leg.

The curtain of fire kept moving closer and First Engineer Vern
Greenlin kept moving back on the fishing boat, until after about
the fifth or sixth attack he was going past the pilot house. Suddenly,
he saw one of the guards jump up and stick his AK-47 inside the
pilot house door and point it right at the head of the helmsman.
"What the hell's going on?" Greenlin asked himself. But he didn't

stop to find out. The Cambodian turned and pointed the AK-47 at Vern, motioning for him to get away from the pilot house. Finally, Greenlin found a nice little protected spot under the overhang on the fantail. Two of the Cambodian guards had already beaten him to it, but he decided to stay anyway. One of the Cambodians was armed with an AK-47, the other with an M-79 grenade-launcher. Vern detested the sight of grenade-launchers. They made him very jittery. Yesterday one of the Cambodians had come down to the engineroom of the *Mayaguez* waving a grenade-launcher around like it was a toy. "Christ almighty," Vern had warned the chief, "if he hits the main steam line with that thing none of us are going to get out of here alive."

Off on the starboard side of the fishing boat, Greenlin saw one of the jets send a white cloud of water into the sky with a rocket. A few seconds later a second jet swooped in and stitched a neat line down the sea with its twenty-millimeter cannon. Either we're going to be blown out of the water or cut in two, Vern thought. Then he looked down and saw a third, even more menacing possibility. The M-79 man's grenade was rolling loose around the fantail, while the guard himself, trying to crawl under the overhang and get away from the flying shrapnel, was kicking it with his feet. Greenlin picked up the grenade. For a second he was tempted to toss it over the stern. But he handed it back to the Cambodian. How long will it take, he wondered, before the pilots up there finally lose patience and blow this fishing boat to pieces. Streaking by at 1,000 miles an hour, he doubted that they could see the white faces up in the bow.

All morning, until about twenty minutes ago, Commander Jim Messegee had been caught in the OPCON radio shack listening to the running report from one or the other of his two Surveillance Birds on station over Koh Tang. It wasn't that the tactical coordinators of either the Skinny Dragon or White Lightning squadrons were overly loquacious. Or that anything very special was going on. Quite the contrary, the birds had been in a regular sea surveillance mode, describing what the electronic sensors and the five pairs of eyes in each cockpit had been picking up.

It was the usual stuff: anti-aircraft fire and its position on the beach; other aircraft on station, and what they were doing; any problems with the aircraft; essentially everything that is routinely connected with the Philippine Air Patrol Group's surveillance role. You might say, that the basic operation this morning involved the same kinds of things the Navy had been doing for many years during the Vietnam war, and for that matter, frequently found itself doing in peacetime, in routine operations such as search and rescue. In any case, the tactical coordinator of each Surveillance Bird had, as was expected of him, been feeding everything back to OPCON at Cubi Point, and into Jim Messegee's ears.

For the last twenty minutes, however, the flow had been reversed. Most of the conversation now was being initiated from Messegee's end. And it was hardly routine, at least not since one of the TAC Birds had broken in on their frequency and said: "I believe I see Caucasian faces." This electrifying news had come immediately after one of Messegee's own Surveillance Birds had twice, and in rapid succession, reported seeing the fishing boat that everybody was eyeballing this morning waver on its course to Kompong Som and try to turn around.

The report of the Caucasian faces had caused Messegee to fire off a fusillade of questions, the most important being: "How many Caucasian faces?" Not that he expected his pilots to go down on the deck and count one, two, three, four, since obviously the lower they went trying to pick out details like that, the more fleeting would be their view of the boat. Besides, that kind of thing was dangerous for Surveillance Birds. Obviously, they made much bigger and slower targets than the speedy little TAC Birds. Still, there were things he needed to know, like what speed was the fishing boat making? How far was she from the Bay of Kompong Som? Were the TAC Birds still trying to turn her around?

The Caucasian faces posed a problem too. They were on a boat moving between Koh Tang and the mainland. And since the order had come from on high last night that the movement of all boats between the island and the mainland, in either direction, be halted, the problem had to be passed to higher authority—possibly to CINCPAC, or to the Pentagon, or who knows, right to the man who issued the order in the first place, the president of the United States.

Jim Messegee glanced at the battery of clocks on the OPCON wall: 2235 Romeo time. For all he knew the president was in bed asleep.

ELEVEN

Calling Pilot to President

IT WAS EIGHT MINUTES after seven, still Tuesday night in Washington, when President Ford left the Oval Office and walked to the residence to have dinner with Betty. He was not aware that at this moment the crew of the *Mayaguez* was on a fishing boat, about to head off for Kompong Som on the Cambodian mainland. But he had been informed that seven gunboats and patrol boats had been observed in the vicinity of the *Mayaguez,* and that the P3 Orion surveillance planes as well as the A-7 Corsairs and F-III fighters, had been drawing heavy machine-gun fire from the boats and shore batteries. At this morning's National Security Council meeting, he had already ordered American planes to prevent any further movement of the gunboats, in either direction, between the *Mayaguez* and the mainland. But now as he walked to the residence he knew that he still had harder decisions to make, perhaps harder than any he had yet made as president. He alone was going to have to choose from the many options available. He'd be lucky, he thought, to get all forty men from the *Mayaguez* back alive. If anything, the Cambodians were becoming more belligerent. Two newly reported ship incidents bore this out. A Thai freighter, the *Eastern Grand,* it was learned, had been seized and held for two hours at Poulo Panjang, forty miles east of where the *Mayaguez* had been captured. The Swedish motor ship *Hirado* had been fired on off the same island, but being fast, had succeeded in outrunning her attackers.

In general terms he talked the problem over with Betty at dinner. While he was back in the residence two telephone calls came from Brent Scowcroft: the first at 8:10, the second at 9:51. But between the two calls, American planes had intercepted seven of the gunboats. The planes, which heretofore had been firing in the water in front of the gunboats to harass them and try to turn them around, had changed tactics, following his orders, and attacked. Three of the gunboats had been sunk, the other four immobilized. An Air Force "Jolly Green Giant," serving as the search and rescue helicopter for the American fighters, had dipped low over the water to try and rescue some of the Cambodian crewmen, but was driven away by gunfire. During the second telephone conversation, which lasted ten minutes—a long call by Ford's standards—the president decided to convene a late-night National Security Council meeting. At 9:59 P.M. he returned from the residence to the Oval Office.

At 10:30 the National Security Council members joined the president in the Cabinet Room. Henry Kissinger, having returned from Missouri an hour earlier, was able to attend.

The president felt certain as the meeting began, that the United States was going to have to move forcefully and fast. The big question was, how much force to use, and the precise moment to use it. More than the crew of the *Mayaguez* was at stake. There was need, particularly after the evacuations of Phnom Penh and Saigon, to dispel doubts about U.S. will and its capacity to respond to provocation.

Kissinger was emphatic on the use of force. He felt that it was important for the American action to have impact on President Kim Il Sung and the North Koreans. The *Pueblo* seizure was on everybody's mind, and so were the most recent North Korean provocations, particularly the tunneling under the thirty-eighth parallel, the border between the North and South. Kissinger wanted whatever action was taken to be read clearly by the North Koreans as well as by the Cambodians. He argued that if Cambodia used the *Mayaguez* crew the way North Korea had used the *Pueblo* crew, it could radically deteriorate the American position in the rest of Asia. Secretary James Schlesinger, on the other hand, stressed the need to recover the ship and punish the Cambodians, but was less eager to use the *Mayaguez* incident as an example for Asia and the world.

President Ford was concerned that once the decision to use force was made, it be sufficient to assure the military success of the operation. He felt a strong personal desire not to err on the side of using too little force. Said the president: "Subjectively, I was having thoughts like this: If it failed and I did nothing, the consequences would be very, very bad, not only in failing to meet that problem, but the implications on a broader international scale. To do something was at least an expression of effort, so I felt it would be far better to take strong action even though the odds might be against us. It was far better than failing and doing nothing."

It was at this meeting that the president decided on the basic strategy for trying to retake the *Mayaguez* and recover the crew. Two Marine units would be used. One unit to assault Koh Tang, and the other to board the *Mayaguez*. Said the president: "We knew by the time of this meeting how quickly the destroyer *Holt* would get there and how soon the destroyer *Wilson* would get there, but we didn't know whether the aircraft carrier *Coral Sea* would be close enough." This was important because the twin-pronged attack would involve air support, including the bombing of selected targets on the mainland.

Actually, five different military options were presented by General David C. Jones, the acting chairman of the Joint Chiefs of Staff. The plan to use the twin-pronged Marine assault coupled with the bombing of selected targets which the president chose, was "option four."

The meeting turned out to be crucial not only from the standpoint of selecting the appropriate action, but in picking the right time as well. As the president, himself, later said: "At this meeting we had all of the contingencies laid out. In fact, there was one operational plan that we would do something before the break of dawn, but we decided to delay even though it meant another twelve to twenty-four hours before we might get there. We didn't know what, of course, would happen in that ten-or twelve-hour span of darkness. But for operational purposes we did delay and lose a little time, and fortunately it turned out well."

The debate over holding up the operation for a day, centered around the availability of the *Coral Sea*. As a former aircraft carrier officer, the president as much as any person present in the Cabinet Room, saw the possible importance of the ship in the rescue of the crew—and the rescue he ruled, above all other objectives, was the primary goal of the military operation.

An exciting crescendo came right in the middle of the meeting, when one of the planes engaged in the action against the Cambodian gunboats, reported an unusual congregation of passengers up near the bow. "I believe I see Caucasian faces," the pilot radioed.

This information was flashed directly to the Situation Room in the White House basement, from where it was rushed up to the Cabinet Room. President Ford described what then transpired: "At the meeting that night we were told there was one boat that we were trying to intercept, or to prevent from getting from the island to the mainland, and the pilot reported that as he went in for his attack, he thought he saw some people on the deck, and rather than sink the boat or strafe it, he asked for instructions. We discussed it at the meeting.

"I had to assume that if this fishing boat, with those crew members, got ashore, that the odds were against us in getting them back. But I was torn with the other side of the coin. If we told the pilot to strafe the boat or sink the boat, that we might be losing everything.

"So it looked like the better decision was to let it proceed, and I issued the order that the pilot should not sink the boat or strafe it. General Scowcroft then went out of the Cabinet Room and down to the Situation Room to carry out the orders. Obviously, the fishing boat got away."

Before the meeting ended the president ordered that the Navy, Marines, and Air Force be put on full alert, capable of moving out in one hour. At 12:25 A.M. President Ford returned to the Oval Office. Ten minutes later he went back to the residence and went to bed.

TWELVE

Gas Attack

THIRD MATE DAVE ENGLISH decided that his hulking 250-pound body presented too big a target for the flying shrapnel, so he moved back from the bow to a spot near the pilot house where the gasoline drums were lined up on deck. After thinking about it, he still wasn't sure whether the jets screaming down on them from behind were trying to turn their fishing boat around, or terrorize the Cambodians to the point where the Americans could seize control. In any case, the pilots' precision was uncanny. As a Marine in Vietnam he knew all about close-air support. But this twenty-millimeter cannon fire was too fucking close. It was spraying the boat with jagged chunks of metal, causing as much pandemonium among the Americans as the Cambodians. English's only fear, though, was that the pilots would finally quit playing around and blow them to kingdom come. Time is running out, he thought. Already, he could see the hazy blue coastline becoming more distinct.

All right, English, he thought. You, Myregard, Friedler—the old man, maybe—you're going to have to grab their guns and do it. You can't have forty different guys deciding what to do. Memories of Vietnam flooded back. One crisp, clear, indelible picture: nineteen young Americans sitting quietly with their hands tied behind their backs, and their heads cut off. Okay, English, two hours from now if you're bleeding to death in some ditch, you'll scream out for another chance like this.

He looked up. Streaking towards them wing-to-wing with the shriek of their jets lagging far behind, he saw two more planes. Suddenly the air above the boat was filled with burning, sizzling objects—little grey cartridges, the size of flashlight batteries, spewing clouds of white gas. English gasped for breath, realizing instantly that was about the stupidest thing he could do. His lungs burned. The fire shot up into his mouth and nose. The skin on his face felt like it was being shredded. "Don't breathe!" he told himself. Back in boot camp at Camp Pendleton he remembered how they had put his drill squad in a gas chamber and made them sing the whole Marine Corps Hymn—"From the Halls of Montezuma to the Shores of Tripoli." But that was only tear gas, not the hot choking chemical rolling over them now in dirty white clouds. He could hear the men around him gasping and coughing, attempting to cry out, because at last they feared the exasperated pilots had swooped in for the kill.

One thing worried English. Not the gas in his lungs. His lungs would clear. But that he would be burned and need medical attention. Most POWs, he knew, died from lack of medicine, not food. Cambodia had no medicine, he was sure.

When the first clouds of gas cleared away, he could see the Cambodians crawling for cover too. The two armed guards on the bow had again laid down their AK-47s and disappeared into the stinking forward fish hatch. The guards standing by the pilot house behind him had their arms wrapped around their faces trying to ward off the burning chemical. "Now's the time," English said to himself. "When the jets strike again I'll be ready."

Wiper Tyrone Matthews had been through the gas chamber, too, only at Fort Polk, Louisiana, and courtesy of the Army and not the Marines. He vividly recalled having to take off his gas mask and give his name, rank, and serial number in a room swirling with tear gas. This gas was different. It burned. So bad in fact that he fought to put his nylon shirt back on and douse the flames which seemed to be consuming his back. Then he grabbed Bayless's jacket and clamped it around his face. Bayless himself was retching down on the deck, more worried though that in the clouds of gas he would lose track of that big ox of an ex-Marine. That wild-assed English is liable to do something stupid in this shit, Bayless thought. He could see the frightened Cambodians crawling around on their hands and knees, coughing and choking like everybody else. He wondered what English was doing.

Cliff Harrington had been standing next to Dave English when the funny little cartridges rained down on the deck. "Look, they're dropping leaflets," he said. Then he caught the first whiff of gas and felt the searing heat in his lungs. I'm going to die, he suddenly thought. But when the gas cleared he nudged English. Two AK-47s were laying unattended, not ten feet in front of them. Beside the guns he also noticed his second engineer, Sanchez, unconscious on the deck.

"Are you OK, Juan?" he called out.

Juan Sanchez had been scared out of his wits, not so much by the piece of shrapnel which had pierced his left ear, as by crazy mutterings he had heard coming from English. The third mate, he feared, was ready to pounce on one of the Cambodians and grab his gun. Sanchez could see the guns blazing and blood streaming all over the deck of the trawler—not just American blood, but Nicaraguan blood too. At that moment, the jets had suddenly swept over the trawler and the gas cartridges were popping in the air, and sizzling all over the deck. Sanchez felt one of the little containers drop inside his coveralls. For a second it burned his stomach. When he glanced down, white smoke was seeping out of his coveralls. "This is the end for me," he said, and he prayed to God for two things. "Let me go to confession, and let me see my daughter, Jeannie, one more time." Then he died—or so he believed.

Before he opened his eyes, Sanchez could hear the chief's voice: "Are you OK, Juan? Are you OK?"

He wasn't sure. His eyes and lungs were scorched, as if somebody had pointed an acetylene torch down his throat and held it there. He opened his eyes and saw the chief holding his head off the deck, wiping his face with a wet rag.

"Are you OK?" the chief asked again.

Sanchez still wasn't sure so he just laid on the deck and breathed the fresh air.

Kassem Saleh, the crew messman, never saw the gas cartridges coming. "I can't breathe. I am burned," he said to himself. "I am sick, I am finished, I am dying." When he came to, Kassem Saleh said: "If they do that again I am going to jump overboard." And Jerry Myregard thought the same thing but for a different reason.

When the gas clouds billowed over the fishing boat, Second Mate Jerry Myregard began to choke and gag like everybody else. But suddenly he realized the gas presented an opportunity. After catching the piece of shrapnel in his right arm, he had moved back to the secluded little shelter deck on the fantail. Vern Greenlin was there too. He glanced over at Vern. He and the two Cambodian guards next to him appeared preoccupied with their own breathing problems. The Cambodians were trying to squeeze into a crawl-space under the deck to get away from the gas.

The jets will be back, Myregard thought. He realized that in the confusion of the attack, and under the white chemical shroud, he could slip over the stern without ever being seen. Nobody'll see me. Even if they do, nobody's going to shout "man overboard." Not with that gas in their lungs. Stay clear of the prop. And stay submerged, he told himself. That's all you have to do.

Myregard started to hyperventilate. It looked perfectly natural. Everybody else was gulping in the fresh air, trying to clear their lungs. He kept taking more air in, letting a little out, then taking another deep breath. He could feel his lungs starting to swell. He glanced at the sweep second hand on his watch.

"OK now. See how long you can hold your breath, Myregard," he said. He held his breath. "One hundred and thirty-three seconds. Not bad." He guessed the speed of the boat was nine knots. "In that time the fishing boat would be six hundred yards away."

Myregard looked over at the coast, now shedding its blue haze, and beginning to show the contour of promontories and coves. Still five or six miles, he thought. Too far. He'd wait until they got closer.

Americo Faria, the big oiler, had come back to the fantail looking for Myregard. Both the second and third mates, he knew, had been talking about grabbing control of the fishing boat away from the Cambodians and heading back to the *Mayaguez*. When the gas attack came Faria got a terrible lungful. At first he thought it was rain. The falling cartridges sounded like rain beating on the water. Then he breathed in the burning gas and thought he was going to die. He prayed to God they'd reach the shore. Finally the air cleared.

"Shit," said Faria. "If they do that one more time they're going to kill us." Suddenly, for no reason at all, he wished he'd sent his fourteen-year-old daughter, Elena, the hundred dollars she had asked for to get her teeth fixed. Elena had sent him a stern-faced snapshot to Hong Kong. "Dear Daddy," she had written. "See, I can't smile for you because I've got holes in my teeth."

When his head finally cleared, Faria realized that the time to grab the Cambodians' guns was during the next gas attack.

"What do you think, Mate?" he asked Myregard, his eyes on the two Cambodians, who were still coughing and snorting from the gas. One had an M-79 grenade-launcher. Faria didn't know how to use that. But the other had an AK-47. That would be easy, he knew.

"Should we take their fucking guns and throw these guys over-board?" he asked Myregard. None of the Cambodians up on the bow would be the wiser. "Nobody can see nothing back here," he said.

Jerry wasn't sure the oiler was serious. He looks serious, he thought. "Not yet," said Myregard. "I'll let you know."

Vern Greenlin was back on the fantail when the gas cartridges fell popping and crackling around him. What the hell's this, he wondered. For an instant he thought the Cambodians must have hit one of the low-flying jets, and that pieces of the exploding plane were falling on the trawler. He hunched down expecting the engines, wings, and fuselage to come hurtling after them. Then he saw the white clouds billow around the boat. He felt sick. He started to retch. Then he reached in his coveralls pocket and pulled out an engineroom rag which he had brought from the *Mayaguez*. He dipped the rag off the stern and held it against his nose. His lungs still burned. But at least he could breathe again. "I'll be ready for the next attack," Greenlin said to himself.

The air cleared and for some reason the jets stayed away. "Thank God, there's no more gas," Third Engineer Alfred Rappenecker said. He still had the captain's handkerchief tied around his right leg under his bloodstained coveralls. He wasn't sure how many pieces of shrapnel were imbedded in his leg, but it throbbed. At least three. Maybe four or five pieces, he thought. He looked out and saw a black channel buoy. Must be getting close to Kompong Som, he thought. Then suddenly more gas cartridges were raining down on the deck.

At first Rappenecker thought his coveralls had caught fire. He rolled on the deck. He couldn't breathe. Then he got up and threw open the pilot house door. He didn't care if the Cambodian guards shot him. He had to get some air. One of the guards yanked him back on deck. He fell down, and dug his hand into the right pocket of his coveralls trying to find the plastic bottle of nitroglycerine capsules. That was one thing he had remembered to bring when they left the *Mayaguez*. He couldn't find the bottle. Finally, he passed out. When he came to, the fishing boat was entering Kompong Som harbor.

Commander Jim Messegee had been hanging close by the OPCON room radio shack while the TAC Birds were trying to turn the fishing boat around. Several times his own Surveillance Birds had reported seeing the boat slow down and start to turn, only to resume its speed and direction.

He had kept his two P3s on station all morning. Both planes could see the TAC Birds swooping low in pairs, laying down the curtain of fire in front of the fishing boat. The TAC Birds were giving it to the boat with rockets and twenty-milli-meter, Messegee knew. But the little boat, his P3s reported, just kept plodding along.

"I'm afraid they realize we're not going to hit them," he said.

One of the TAC Birds had offered to try and shoot the rudder off the boat. That idea was nixed. Too chancy. The president himself had ordered that the fishing boat should not be fired on.

Next the TAC Birds had gone in with gas. That didn't stop the boat either.

Technically, his Surveillance Birds were maintaining twelve-mile CPA—as the "closest point of approach" to the Cambodian coast was referred to around the OPCON room. But now that those "Caucasian faces" had been spotted on the fishing boat, Messegee knew the P3s would move in closer to shore. "If the Cambodians take those men ashore," Messegee said to Brandt Powell, his exec, "we've kinda lost the ball game."

He didn't say it, but he felt that once the Americans set foot on the Cambodian mainland the chances of ever recovering them were indeed remote. "It would be a terrible gamble to have to go in there and get them back," he said.

All morning there were two imponderables lurking in the back of Messegee's mind. Did those "Caucasian faces" represent the entire *Mayaguez* crew? Part of the crew could have stayed back in Koh Tang. Or for that matter, back on the *Mayaguez* itself.

Then there was the second question. If the Cambodians got the crew over to the mainland, did that mean the gunboats would go back out and try to blow up the *Mayaguez* before the U.S. destroyers could tow it away?

Messegee hung right by the radio shack waiting for the word. Finally it came. The TAC Birds had failed. They couldn't stop the fishing boat. Not even with gas. The boat was now entering Kompong Som harbor.

THIRTEEN

"Welcome to Cambodia," He Said

CHARLIE MILLER COULDN'T remember when he'd felt worse. The gas had cleared from his lungs, but his brain was still fogged. He was looking up at a bulkhead thirty feet higher than the deck of their fishing boat, into the faces of 500 Cambodians—grim, staring, unflinching faces.

He stared back. There were men, women, and children. All in black pajamas. Almost all armed, even the women and children. Their black eyes peered down at Charlie and his crew squashed together on the bow of the fishing boat as if they were some prize catch about to be flung up on the dock for the crowd's adulation.

"You dumb sonofabitch," he said to himself. "You let them trick you. The little pricks never did plan to take you back to the ship."

The fishing boat backed off from the bulkhead, turned, and nestled port-to-starboard alongside another fishing boat which was tied to a small wooden pier. The other fishing boat, Charlie noticed, was flying a Viet Cong flag. Off to his right, two Chinese freighters were berthed end-to-end and unloading sacks of rice on a long concrete pier. "Wharf number two," he thought. The dock in Kompong Som where the Cambodian ensign kept trying to make him bring the *Mayaguez*.

Now what? he wondered. March us down the street and let everybody look? Behind the crowd he could see an open square: faded yellow buildings, a few ramshackle shops, and a storage shed.

The crowd kept growing—more men, women, and children come to ogle the Caucasian captives.

Vern Greenlin eyed the armed crowd and thought of the three *Pueblo* crewmen who lived in Santa Rosa. For a while they had been hometown celebrities. Now everybody had forgotten about their eleven months' captivity in North Korea. Why don't they get it over with, he thought. March us through the city and let everybody throw shit at us. Isn't that what they do?

Dave English looked over at the two Chinese freighters with the red stars and lightning flashes on their stacks. A few of the Chinese sailors stood on the deck staring at the fishing boat full of Americans. He tried to read their expressions. Not that they were inscrutable, just too far away. He tried to read the home ports painted on the sterns. Canton and Tientsin, he thought, but he wasn't sure. For some reason it occurred to him that if the Cambodians were going to keep the *Mayaguez,* they might send the crew back to Hong Kong on a Chinese freighter.

"English, who are you kidding?" he said. "It's going to be the old march up the street to prison like it was for the American pilots in Hanoi." He could see it: the *Kompong Som Hilton,* if they didn't get their heads chopped off first.

Juan Sanchez glanced over at the other fishing boat, and saw a dozen more armed guards ready to take them away. He had never stopped praying since the jets had dropped the gas. "Dear God," he said, "let me go to confession, and see Jeannie one more time."

Jerry Myregard was still having trouble understanding his own stupidity. "Two chances to escape and you blew them both," he said. His eyes fastened on the AK-47s slung over so many slender shoulders. It didn't seem likely there would be another chance.

Tyrone Matthews let his discriminating eye rove over the crowd and found it full of girls. The one standing in the door of that army trailer with her family was a pretty cute chick, he thought. She reminded him of a chick in Saigon, whom he had once stopped to talk to in the street, when some pimp with a tire iron came along and hit him in the face. The chick, he found out, had owed the pimp some money.

Gerardo Lopez kept turning his head and surveying the port of Kompong Som. No, he was sure. This was not the place in Cambodia where they had been hit by rockets on the *Steel Traveller*. That was another place.

Gerald Bayless could only think of the *Pueblo*. He looked at all the armed men peering down at him and thought, it could be years before we go free.

Burt Coombes saw all the men in black pajamas and wondered which one was the military commander who must be there to meet them. Then he saw all the guns. I don't care if they shoot us, he thought, as long as they don't beat us with their rifle butts.

Alfred Rappenecker still felt woozy from the gas attack. He clutched at the breast pocket of his coveralls searching again for the nitroglycerine capsules. He found them. Better get some water and take one now. Then he looked up and saw the crowd. They're all young, he thought, nobody's as old as me.

Americo Faria felt happy to be alive. If they gassed us one more time we'd be dead, he thought. The little people in black on the dock didn't scare him. I'll just let the captain do the talking.

Charlie Miller wondered if by some chance the next move could be up to him. A dozen or so additional armed guards had materialized, and they stood on the deck of the fishing boat jabbering with the guards who had escorted them from Koh Tang. Nobody seemed to know what to do. Maybe they're afraid to march us past that armed mob, he thought. The mob, he noticed, had doubled in size in the last fifteen minutes. Well, I'm the captain. Maybe I should demand to speak with a representative of the Khmer Rouge government. Then he looked out and saw a gunboat entering the harbor.

The gunboat, number 133, made a wide sweep and pulled up alongside their fishing boat. A brief exchange between their guards and the gunboat crew ensued, and suddenly the fishing boat's lines were being cast off. Where the hell are we going now, Charlie wondered. Baie de Ream?

The fishing boat purred out of Kompong Som harbor, turned left and proceeded southeast, paralleling the coast for about fifteen minutes. When it came abeam of a white sand beach, it turned left again, and anchored 100 yards from the shore. Behind the beach, Charlie could see what appeared to be a prison compound nestled in among the trees. The cement buildings faced out onto a small parade ground. Many of the windows were barred. An archway wreathed with barbed wire provided entry to the compound.

"I guess that's our new home," Charlie said to Cliff Harrington who had come up beside him on the bow of the fishing boat.

"Looks like it," answered the chief, peering over at the prison compound.

On the beach Charlie could see two men trying to slide a large dory over the sand down to the water. But the dory was too heavy, so the men walked back towards a creek to look for another boat that was already launched. "I guess those men are coming to get us," he said. "Say, Chief," he blurted suddenly, "if I don't make it back to the *Mayaguez,* I want you to know there's sixteen thousand nine hundred fifty-three dollars hidden under the left drawer of my bunk."

"Why don't we say the Cambodians took it," said the chief. "You and I can split it."

"You serious?" asked Charlie.

"No. But it's not a bad idea. Charlie, what makes you think I'm going to get out of here if you don't?"

The rest of the *Mayaguez* crew had lapsed into silence. Even Friedler had shut up. Charlie guessed that the flying shrapnel, the gas, and the dynamite sun beating down on their heads for the last six hours, had turned off the conversation. He could see that the sun had cooked Dave English the color of rare roast beef. Sanchez and Rappenecker looked sick. Myregard's right arm still oozed blood. And Charlie, since he had seen all those armed Cambodians standing up on the bulkhead in Kompong Som, didn't feel very well himself. The chief, he knew, was just trying to cheer him up.

"I *was* serious, Cliff. I'm sixty-two years old. Maybe I won't get back to the ship."

He glanced over at the shore. The two men who had been trying to launch the dory had now located another boat. But they were having severe problems coordinating their rowing. First one would yank on his oar, then the other, as the dory came zigging and zagging out from shore. The action was diverting enough that Charlie failed to see the fishermen on his own boat start passing out food. When he turned around one of the fishermen was standing there with a big iron pot of rice and ten or twelve enameled tin bowls. But before he served Charlie his rice, he crossed his wrists a couple of times and pointed to himself. Charlie thought the fisherman was merely being friendly.

"I guess he feels sorry for us," Charlie said to Cliff. "He's trying to tell me to eat before they handcuff us and haul us away."

Gerald Bayless had been standing there next to Charlie watching the little pantomime scene being acted out by the fisherman. "This guy don't look Cambodian to me," he announced. "I think he's a Thai."

Bayless liked to spend his vacations down in Pattaya, a Thai beach resort south of Bangkok. In fact, he still had a thousand dollars on deposit in the Asia Trust Bank there, which he had been meaning to go back and get. "The Thais are a different breed of cat," he said. "They don't look like Cambodians."

Charlie didn't doubt Bayless. He just didn't know what the hell difference it made whether the fishermen turned out to be Thais, as long as the guys in the boat with the guns, were Cambodians. He studied the food which the Thai or Cambodian, or whatever he was, had put in his bowl. It offered no clue of nationality: steamed rice with some kind of green shoots. The greens looked like marsh grass, except for the tiny pale buds on top. The Cambodian guards didn't touch the food. Charlie had already noticed that whenever a gunboat came alongside, the guards would be handed a green leaf with rice wrapped inside.

The two men zigzagging out from shore in the rowboat finally made it. Here we go, thought Charlie. They're going to ferry us over to the beach, a couple at a time, and lock us up in that compound.

But it turned out the rowers had no reason for coming. The men were unarmed, and as far as Charlie could tell, they had simply come out to get a closer look at this curious collection of foreigners caught by the fishermen. For a few minutes the two men rested on their oars, then they zigzagged back to shore just as gunboat 133 reappeared. Another lively discussion ensued between the gunboat crew and the armed guards on the fishing boat. Finally, the fishermen pulled up their anchor and the two boats took off in tandem headed in a westerly direction. High off to the left, Charlie could see the black specks of two American reconnaissance planes combing the coastline.

A ripple of chatter ran through the *Mayaguez* crew. Charlie could hear the buzz of rumors travel back towards the pilot house of the fishing boat, and return in a completely different form. "We're going back to the ship," is the way the rumor started out. "We're headed for the Thai border," is the way it came back.

The Thai border makes sense, he thought. It's only eighty miles away. Once they get rid of us, they can go out and get the *Mayaguez* and bring her into wharf number two. He had noticed two tugs in Kompong Som harbor. They don't need us, he thought. They can tow the ship into wharf number two. What they really want is our cargo.

"The truth is," Charlie said to himself, "nobody knows where the fuck we're going. I wonder if the Cambodians do?"

They ran due west for an hour and a half to an island he recognized as Koh Rong Sam Lem. Two islands, he remembered from the "Ko Kut to Baie de Ream" chart, sit in the gaping mouth of the Bay of Kompong Som, helping to shelter it. Koh Rong, about ten miles long, is the main island. Koh Rong Sam Lem, about five miles long and shaped, he recalled, like a kitten with its nose pointing to sea and its tail pointing to shore, is the smaller island. He watched the fishing boat turn left into a glittering emerald bay enclosed between the kitten's front and back paws. If Koh Rong Sam Lem, was in the Caribbean, Charlie suddenly thought, it would be called an island paradise and caught in a stampede of cruise ships. Lush green hills slanted down to a white ring of rock and sand. He glanced at his watch: 2:15.

"They're sure salting us away in a remote spot, Charlie," Cliff Harrington said. "I think they're trying to hide us from our own jets." The chief engineer had already concluded that the Cambodians were going to go out and sink the *Mayaguez*, then negotiate with the United States for the release of the crew.

"The guys who survive this," he said, "will be the ones who can stand the gaff of the jungle." Cliff had been thinking about the *Pueblo* ever since they arrived in Kompong Som. "You'll see, Charlie. Ten or twelve months from now, maybe we'll get out of here."

Across the bay, nestled under a dense jungle backdrop, Charlie could see the delicate filigree of a fishing village built on stilts. From a distance the village looked like it was made of matchsticks. But as they drew closer he could see the unique construction: dried banana-leaf roofs, bamboo walls perched atop teakwood pilings, with a spider web of elevated split-bamboo boardwalks linking all the buildings together. Finally, as they approached the dock, he noticed just how substantial the buildings were: fifteen or twenty large permanent sheds, built over the water to house some kind of a mill or foundry. Gunboat 133 had already tied up. Two more gunboats lay against the dock. Both of them had been crudely camouflaged. Nets covered with dried shrimps had been draped over their pilot houses. Crude or not, a speeding jet would have trouble picking them out, Charlie thought. Another fishing boat was parked there too.

The tide was high. Charlie stood on the gunwhale of the fishing boat, and even for him it was only a short step up to the dock. A young man in typical native dress—black pajamas, a red plaid bandana tied around his head, and sandals—stood on the dock. He carried no gun. His right hand was extended, and he was smiling.

"Welcome to Cambodia," he said.

Fortunately for Charlie, he always did have a gift for taking things as they came. Or maybe there just were no more surprises left for this orphan boy turned jockey, who quit the track for the sea, and worked his way up to captain before being captured in Cambodia. But Charlie Miller could think of only one thing to say.

"I'm Captain Miller," he said.

In clear and understandable English the man continued. "We'll go ashore and have some hot tea. Then we'll fix some food."

The man led Charlie through half a dozen large buildings connected by the split-bamboo walkways which Charlie had observed from out on the bay. One of the buildings, he could now see, appeared to have been a sawmill, another some kind of a smelter for tin or lead. Inside were the blackened crucibles, iron cauldrons, brick ovens, and charred bamboo. Between the buildings Charlie found that he had to walk sideways to keep his feet from slipping between the slats.

Finally they reached the shore where the rest of the village, consisting of thirty or forty more buildings, sat in a jungle clearing surrounded by banana, papaya, and coconut trees. Eggplant lined the pathways. Pigs and chickens scampered in and out of the dense thicket. And behind the village, the jungle rose abruptly to the top of a seven-hundred-foot hill.

One large building with a red flag flying from it, the man indicated, would be off limits to the *Mayaguez* crew. Otherwise they could have the run of the village. Charlie observed black-pajamaed men coming and going from this building. It looked like a barracks, which from its size he guessed would hold fifty or sixty men. It took a while to sink in. But one thing became apparent. There were no women in this village. The village, explained the man, was the compound of the Second Military Command of Kompong Som. The First Military Command was in Kompong Som proper. The High Command, as he called it, was in Phnom Penh.

The man, whom Charlie had come to think of as the "English-speaker"—because he wasn't sure if he was the local commander —led Charlie into a large one-room building with a mud floor and with chickens rooting around inside it. The pigs, Charlie saw very soon, were also privileged to wander in and out. A table, large enough to seat four or five people on each side, had been placed in the center of the room. Along the walls were king-sized cots, about double the width of standard American Army cots. Styrofoam mattresses lay scattered over the mud floor. Cliff Harrington followed Charlie into the building. Several of the crew instinctively tagged along, until Charlie made it clear that he, accompanied by the chief, was going to do all the talking. Vern Greenlin dropped down on one of the styrofoam mattresses, and as far as Charlie could tell, fell instantly asleep.

"Sit down here," the English-speaker said, pointing to the big table which had a bench on each side. A porcelain pitcher, a teapot, and a one-gallon can of coarse white sugar lay on the table.

"Which would you like? Tea or sweet water?" the English-speaker asked. Charlie and the chief took tea. The English-speaker poured two glasses of pale green tea, hot and steaming, into two tall jelly glasses. He poured himself a glass of hot water and ladled in some sugar. Then he got down to business.

"Do any members of your crew work for the CIA?" he asked. Over in a corner of the big room, Charlie could see Sereno and a couple of the crew hacking away at coconuts with a borrowed machete. Those fellas CIA? he thought.

"No. We have no CIA men on the *Mayaguez*," he answered.

"Are any of your crew members of the FBI?" the English-speaker asked next.

"No," said Charlie. "We're all merchant sailors. Nobody works for the United States government."

Apparently the English-speaker had a regular checklist of questions all set in his mind. He was running down the list. "Do you have any electronic equipment aboard your ship?"

"Only our radar," said Charlie. "All American merchant vessels are equipped with radar. It is standard equipment. Only ours is broken." Sereno walked across the room and offered Charlie and the chief a drink of coconut milk. Charlie took a couple of quick sips, but he didn't want to interrupt the flow of questions, hoping that his interrogator would finally reveal what disposition Cambodia planned to make of him and the *Mayaguez* crew. Entering the building, he could not help but notice one member of the black pajama squad shaving banana stalks with an enormous broad-bladed knife. The man was mixing the shavings with some kind of meal and feeding it to the pigs. But the knife was what had caught Charlie's attention. It was the kind of cleaver he could visualize the Cambodians using to chop heads. Not that the English-speaker wasn't the model of politeness, calling Charlie "Captain" and putting him at his ease. Still, Charlie thought, there was always the possibility that the Cambodians might try to make an example out of one man.

The English-speaker continued in his courteous vein. "What is your cargo?" he asked.

"General cargo," Charlie answered. The truth was he didn't precisely know what was in his 274 containers. Ninety were empty. He knew that. The rest, he assumed, contained spare parts, frozen foods, PX supplies, and personal effects for the 25,000 U.S. military personnel and their dependents still based in Thailand. But he wasn't sure. When the U.S. Military Sea Command contracts with commercial steamship companies such as Sea-Land Service, Inc., it simply lists "military equipment" or "NOS," meaning "not oth-

erwise specified," on the ship's manifest. On the other hand if the
ship had been carrying ammunition or explosives, the kinds of
cargo the English-speaker was concerned about, Charlie would
have been informed. All high risk cargoes, he knew, required special handling and special insurance.

"What is in your general cargo?" asked the English-speaker.

"Cabbages, apples, oranges, frozen chicken and beef, cotton
shirts, socks, and toothpaste," answered Charlie. Charlie was trying to be truthful. But he had already decided not to mention
Sattahip, their next port of call, since it was widely known to
supply the U.S. military establishment in Thailand. "The kind of
cargo that merchants buy in ports like Bangkok and Singapore to
sell to the general public," Charlie added, perhaps conveying a
picture of the *Mayaguez* participating in some great dockside ba-
zaar. Then he explained how the *Mayaguez* served only as a feeder
vessel in Asia, that it never went back to the United States to load,
and as a matter of course carried no guns, ammunition, or electronic equipment. The English-speaker, Charlie thought, seemed
to be convinced that he was telling the truth.

"From your ship," asked the English-speaker, "can you talk to
the American planes?"

For an instant Charlie considered admitting that the *Mayaguez*
had sent off an SOS when it was fired on by the Cambodian
gunboat. But he decided not to. "No," he said. "We can only talk
to commercial radio stations or to other ships."

"But then why did so many planes come?" asked the English-
speaker. "Three of our boats have been sunk and one hundred
friendly Cambodian people have been hurt."

This was big news. Possibly bad news, too, and it resurrected
thoughts of the man shaving banana stalks outside with the guillo-
tine-sized knife. But Charlie seized on two hopeful signs. The
English-speaker had omitted mentioning any fatalities. He had also
spoken without animosity, as if it were some third-country nation-
als, and not Charlie's own countrymen, who were wreaking havoc

on Cambodia. Charlie suddenly saw hope that Cambodia's fear of further destruction might help in their release.

"You have to understand," he said, "the *Mayaguez* was scheduled to reach Thailand at nine o'clock yesterday morning. When the ship failed to arrive, naturally they sent planes out to look for it."

"Is there no way you can contact the American planes?" the English-speaker asked.

"There is only one way," Charlie explained. "If we go back to the ship, get steam up, and start the generators so we have electricity, then we can call our office in Bangkok. The office can contact the American authorities." He decided not to mention that the ship carried emergency batteries for the single sideband transmitter.

The English-speaker had been jotting a few sketchy notes. Now he wanted numbers. How many men were needed to get steam up? How long would it take? How soon after he had steam could Charlie contact his Bangkok office? How long would it then take to stop the planes?

The English-speaker made no attempt to conceal the urgency of the situation. The presence of the lethal supersonic jets had clearly come as a shock. The English-speaker got on to other questions, but he kept coming back to the planes. He mentioned "bombings" and "targets" which Charlie knew nothing about.

The interrogation went on for an hour. Finally, Charlie was asked to supply the names and jobs of all the crew members. He wrote them down. In return the English-speaker explained his own military hierarchy. He, himself, was twenty-eight years old and merely the interpreter. The thirty-two-year-old compound commander, whom Charlie would soon meet, was also second-in-command of the entire Kompong Som district. Charlie suspected the English-speaker might be the real boss. He seemed so clean-cut and smart, the kind of young mate Charlie Miller always liked to get aboard ship.

"Now," said the Cambodian, "I will show you where you sleep. He led Charlie outside. Wilfredo Reyes, the Filipino electrician was swinging from the treetops knocking down coconuts for the other crew members. But everybody quickly followed the captain back across the elevated bamboo walkway.

"How long we going to stay here, Captain?" asked Omer the messman, who was still wearing his white jacket. Omer had purposely kept on his messman's jacket when the Cambodians took him ashore. Nobody will shoot me, he had reasoned. They'll think my jacket is a white flag.

"I don't know, Omer," answered Charlie. The captain looks worried, Omer thought. And that made Omer worry even more.

When they reached the first big building sitting up on stilts, the English-speaker motioned for Charlie to go inside. "This is where you will sleep," he said.

The quarters were spacious enough—a large covered veranda with a split-bamboo deck extending about fifteen feet out over the water. There were a couple of hammocks, a few more of those king-sized cots Charlie had seen in the other building, and several styrofoam mattresses. The space would easily accomodate the forty-man crew, as long as most of them slept on the bamboo slats. In one corner was an office. This, the English-speaker indicated, was shared by him and his commander. It contained two bunks and a table. On the table Charlie could see a U.S. Army fieldpack radio —the Khmer Rouge must have captured a whole warehouse full of these American radios, he thought—some extra batteries, a Coleman lantern minus its mantle, and a can with a wick sticking out of it, which obviously was now being used to substitute for the lantern.

"Sit down," said the English-speaker, motioning to one of the cots in his small private room. On the veranda, large iron pots were already being brought out for dinner. Everybody was invited to dig in, although a shortage of bowls and spoons was going to necessitate eating in three or four shifts. Charlie decided to wait. The compound commander had just arrived, and he and Charlie and the English-speaker launched into a three-way conversation about the American planes. The commander also wanted to know if Charlie had the ability to make radio contact with the planes to stop the bombing. The commander spoke no English. Charlie could see he was a little older than the English-speaker. He looked a lot less friendly.

Finally Charlie was handed a bowl and spoon. The two Cambodians insisted on waiting until all of the Americans had eaten. Charlie filled his bowl with rice. Then he sampled what appeared to be pickled eggplant, which was supposed to be poured over the rice. It burned his lips. "Whew! Too hot for me," he exclaimed. Instead he ladled some chicken broth with a couple of neckbones in it, over his rice. Charlie ate the rice and dropped the neckbones between the bamboo slats. The tide had gone out and the bones bounced off the rocks below.

Third Mate Dave English had been hanging around hoping to horn in on the captain's conversation. It wasn't that he didn't trust the old man to do the negotiating for all of them. But he knew the captain had a lot on his mind. "Anyway, you can't expect the old man to think of everything," he had told himself. What English really wanted to find out was how long they were going to be holed up in that mosquito-infested jungle hideout. He already had huge bites all over his badly sunburned arms and legs. When he saw the captain get up and head for the pots of food, he pounced.

The young Cambodian was friendly enough. "Are you married?" he asked English.

"Yes," said the third mate. "To an Asian girl. A Filipina."

The Cambodian smiled, then changed the subject. "Why did the Americans permit Lon Nol to live in Hawaii?" he asked.

"It wasn't that we liked Lon Nol, or disliked Lon Nol," said English. "We just don't like to see anybody get killed." The Cambodian, he noticed, did not take offense. This emboldened English to try nudging the conversation around to how long the Cambodians might detain them. But he couldn't get the young man to bite. Finally English blurted it out: "How long are you going to keep us prisoners?" he asked.

"Two months, possibly," answered the Cambodian. "First we will take you to Kompong Som. They will decide. But you must stop the bombing before they will let you go."

English could feel anger adding heat to his big sunburned body. He wanted to reach out and shake the little Cambodian until his neck snapped. "We can't stop the bombing if we're stuck here," he bellowed.

Charlie Miller caught the third mate's bellow from across the veranda. He came charging back to the English-speaker's room. "I'll be the spokesman for this group," he said to English. "You just keep quiet." English's temper flashes were familiar to Charlie. But he knew they dissipated fast. Like Charlie's old friend Captain Abe Waldman, English had a way of blowing up and calming down instantly. After that he would be friendly as ever.

Charlie and Abe Waldman had been ABs together on the old *President Taft*. Back in those days all the quartermasters slept in one cabin and all the ABs in another. One night in Hong Kong Charlie had come rolling back aboard ship a little fired up on rice wine. He tossed a lighted firecracker under Abe Waldman's bunk. It was one of those big double-barrel salutes used by the Chinese to scare off evil spirits. The first explosion blew Abe Waldman out of his bunk. By the time the second barrel exploded Waldman had belted Charlie in the mouth. Waldman had big thumbnails and the blow cut Charlie's upper lip in two. Waldman then felt so sorry for Charlie he took him down to the doctor at three o'clock in the morning to get his lip sewn back together.

That's the way English was. The wild bull of a third mate immediately turned gentle as a lamb. "All right, Captain," he said. Charlie watched him walk over to a cot and promptly fall asleep.

The light was beginning to fade. Out through the open veranda

Charlie could see the verdant, precipitous hillside start to purple. The English-speaker picked up the fieldpack radio and started calling Kompong Som. He and the compound commander took turns talking. When the conversation ended the English-speaker announced that Charlie and three of his crewmen would return to the *Mayaguez* to get steam up and the generators going, so they could call on the radio and stop the bombing.

"Three men are not enough," said Charlie. The Cambodian didn't argue. He picked up the fieldpack radio and talked to Kompong Som again. "All right," he said, "you can take seven men."

Charlie got the chief. "How many men do you need to get the plant going, Cliff?" he asked.

Harrington considered the problem. It's been more than twenty-four hours since we shut down. But it was hot outside. Without the blowers going he guessed it would be 130 or 140 degrees down there. Better figure on two shifts. "Seven, Captain," he said.

Charlie wanted Myregard, the second mate, to go too, and of course Sparks had to go to operate the radio. The numbers kept building. "I'll need nine men plus myself," Charlie said.

The English-speaker didn't hesitate. "All right," he said.

Cliff Harrington, rarin' to get out of the boondocks of Cambodia and back to his ship, was the first man down on the dock. The fishing boat was still there and the crew was still on it. But for some reason the fishermen indicated they couldn't go.

"Thailand," said one of the fishermen pointing to himself. Then he crossed his wrists, just the way one of the other fishermen had done for Charlie earlier. "Prisoner," he said. "Me prisoner." He held up five fingers. Cliff thought the man meant he had been captured five days ago. "Five months," the fisherman said.

"Jesus Christ," Harrington said. "Five months! I hope they don't keep us five months."

Charlie Miller, walking sideways again, so his small shoes wouldn't slip between the bamboo slats of the elevated walkway, had been accompanied to the dock by the English-speaker. A gunboat was just tying up as they arrived.

"This boat will bring you back to your ship," said the English-speaker.

Jerry Myregard eyed the gunboat. Then he glanced up at the jungle rising steeply behind the village. He had studied that terrain carefully this afternoon and had already picked his escape route over the heavily thicketed hill. The sudden decision to send him back to the *Mayaguez* had come as a reprieve. But suddenly he changed his mind. "Captain, you can go without me," he said. "I'm not going by gunboat. Our own planes will blow that thing out of the water."

"You can wait," said the English-speaker. "Another fishing boat will come in half an hour."

Charlie looked at his watch: 6:30. "It'll be dark long before we get to the ship," he said. "Even the fishing boat will be dangerous in the dark." But he knew how anxious the Cambodians were for him to go. He didn't expect the English-speaker to agree.

The young Cambodian put his hand on Charlie's shoulder. "Wait till morning," he said. "Then you can all go." Charlie wondered if he had understood the English-speaker correctly. Did he mean the whole crew?

Dave English had been roused out of his nap by a fire. One of the cooks had kicked over an aluminum box which he had been using as a homemade kerosene stove, and the whole shed started to go up in flame. English joined in the bucket brigade, helping to douse the fire. And as it turned out, he did another good deed. One of the sentries, he noticed, was toting around an M-79 grenade-launcher with a cracked bore. Ex-Marine English knew what would happen if the man fired his weapon. It would blow up in his face. So he stopped the sentry, and using sign language, got his point across. The sentry seemed pleased by English's concern, and he thanked him. This had made English feel slightly better about their own predicament. Of course, he was pissed off not to be picked by Captain Miller to go back to the *Mayaguez*. The old man's probably mad at me, he thought. But English had gotten over his pique. When he looked out and saw Charlie Miller and the nine handpicked guys coming back from the dock, he really blew his stack. Right away, he knew the Cambodians had screwed them again. "More of their fucking lies," he bellowed. "It's just a bunch of bullshit. They're not going to let anybody go back to the ship."

Tyrone Matthews, Darryl Kastl, and Pantryman Pastrano were walking back from the shore side of the village, when they spotted the skipper and the others coming back from the dock. "That's beautiful," said Matthews. "We're going to stay. This is a jungle paradise."

Over in the village, Kastl had found a medal. It was shaped like Buddha. "It looks Thai," Matthews said. "I don't think it's Cambodian." Kastl stuck the medal in his pocket.

Pastrano had come upon a small plastic bag of tobacco. "Great, man," said Matthews, "everybody's out of butts." Matthews then found a Khmer Rouge propaganda booklet. The three men ripped out the pages and rolled themselves some cigarettes. On the way back to their sleeping quarters Matthews met a young Cambodian who could speak a little English. He told Matthews that he had gotten a good look at one of the American planes. Close enough, he said, so he could read the number. It was number 105. Matthews wondered if he meant it was an F-105. He's a country boy, Matthews thought.

Anastacio Sereno had eaten a lot of rice and greens because he wasn't sure where his next meal was going to come from. The food was spicy and his stomach burned. The mosquitoes bothered him too. "We have big mosquitoes in the Philippines," he said, "but not this big."

Gerardo Lopez had found a straw mat to sleep on, but one of the Cambodian guards brought him a styrofoam mattress. He was just dozing off when he saw the captain and the nine men coming from the dock. Lopez was convinced they would not leave this camp alive. My first voyage was to Cambodia, he thought. And so is my last.

When Charlie Miller got back to the place they were supposed to sleep, he found the rest of the crew had picked all the good spots. Charlie laid down on the slats and tried to sleep. The English-speaker had warned that nobody was to go outside or he might be shot. Charlie could see the black figures of the sentries passing quietly as panthers up and down the split-bamboo boardwalks in the dark. He still wondered what the English-speaker meant when he said: "Wait till morning. Then you can all go."

Maybe we'll never go, he thought. You could never tell. A lot could happen between now and morning. Well, there still were a couple of things he wanted to do. Like see his two children. Fifteen years since he'd seen Jimmy and Cheryl. For all he knew they had children of their own by now.

"That you down there, Cap?" he heard a voice say. He looked up from the floor and saw one of the crew sitting on the edge of a cot: Pantryman Pastrano, he thought.

"Cap, you want to share a cigarette with me?"

Pastrano, he knew, had found a bag of Cambodian tobacco and some newspaper to roll it in. But it tasted worse than corn silk. "No, thanks," he said.

"How come? It's a good one, Cap. It's a Winston."

Charlie sat up on the edge of Pastrano's bunk and they took drags together on the Winston. "You don't need to sleep down there, Cap," Pastrano said. "I can slide over and we'll both sleep."

FOURTEEN

The Commander in Chief's Gamble

ALTHOUGH PRESIDENT FORD had been kept late in the Cabinet Room at the National Security Council meeting and had not gotten to bed until 1 A.M., he was up at his customary 5:30 A.M. rising hour. As he completed his morning exercises the president pondered the various fates which might have now befallen the *Mayaguez* crew. The pilot said that he *"believed"* he had seen Caucasian faces on the fishing boat which finally vanished into Kompong Som harbor. It was not a certainty. But in any case it made the handling of the crisis more dangerous. As the president said: "We had to assume a whole variety of possibilities because we weren't sure if there were crew members on the fishing boat, and if so how many there were, and how many were back on the *Mayaguez.*" There was also the good chance that some of the men were on Koh Tang, the island just one mile from where the *Mayaguez* lay anchored, and thirty-four miles from the mainland.

But the best possibility was that at least some of the crew were on the mainland. And in that case, since six hours had now passed since their arrival in Kompong Som, they could already be in Phnom Penh, or almost any place inside Cambodia. Prospects of making a quick and full recovery of the crew appeared very dim to President Ford early Wednesday morning.

At 6 A.M. Dr. William Lukash, the president's physician, went up to the living quarters and found the president sitting in his shorts reading a newspaper. The doctor reminded him that he had a 7:15 A.M. dental appointment to have his teeth cleaned. Since President Ford had gotten to bed late, Dr. Lukash suggested that he might want to postpone it. The president kept the dental appointment, nevertheless arriving on schedule at 7:40 in the Oval Office.

At 7:44 General Brent Scowcroft entered to give the president his morning briefing. He had very little new information on the *Mayaguez*. There was one favorable item. Headwinds which had been slowing the aircraft carrier *Coral Sea*, had subsided. Said the president: "They made better time when the night came, so by morning we knew that the *Coral Sea* could be utilized rather than relying on other air strikes." The president appreciated the flexibility the *Coral Sea* would add to the military operations ready to be implemented. The session with General Scowcroft was concluded in twenty-one minutes.

Three times before lunch, Secretary Kissinger popped into the Oval Office for short meetings with the president. There were several diplomatic problems to discuss in connection with the *Mayaguez*. No answers to the notes delivered to the Chinese or to the Cambodian representatives in Peking had been received. Letters to United Nations Secretary General Kurt Waldheim and to the UN Security Council were being prepared. Then there was also the matter of the Thai government's publicly expressed anger at the presence of U.S. Marines, which had erupted into anti-American demonstrations in Bangkok. Besides, though it had no connection with the *Mayaguez*, the president had to prepare for his meetings with the Netherlands' premier, Joop M. den Uyl, to discuss the NATO summit conference to be held in the first week of June.

During the morning, the White House liaison men were making calls to inform congressional leaders that U.S. forces had struck gunboats off the Cambodian coast and had sunk three and damaged four. (No public announcement had yet been made of the gunboat sinkings.) The White House had not previously advised congressional leaders specifically that the bombing of the gunboats was contemplated, only that attempts would be made to intercept any gunboats apprehended moving in either direction between the *Mayaguez* and the mainland.

At 10:15 President Ford met with a group of Michigan business-men for fifteen minutes in the White House theater. Following that he met for an hour with Premier den Uyl of the Netherlands.

At 1 P.M. the president presided over a meeting of his economic and domestic policy advisors, at which it was decided to reject the New York City appeal for financial aid. At the same time in New York City, John Scali, the U.S. ambassador to the United Nations, took the elevator up to Kurt Waldheim's office and presented a letter asking the secretary general to take any steps within his ability to effect the immediate release of the *Mayaguez,* as well as its crew, seized by Cambodian gunboats in the Gulf of Thailand. The letter warned that: "in the absence of a positive response to our appeal . . . my government reserves the right to take measures as may be necessary to protect the lives of American citizens and property." Later in the day a second letter was delivered to the United Nations, this one addressed to the Security Council. It recapitulated the details of the ship's seizure. According to this letter, which gave the latitude and longitude of the *Mayaguez,* the ship was on the high seas and in international shipping lanes. Even if it were considered by Cambodia to be within its country's ter-ritorial waters, the *Mayaguez,* said the letter: "would clearly have been engaged in innocent passage to the port of another country."

In ordering that these letters be sent to the United Nations, the president knew that the chances of effective UN action was nil. Kurt Waldheim's previous communications to the new Cambodian regime, whether sent to Phnom Penh or to the exiled Prince Noro-dom Sihanouk in Peking, had received no response. Also, the president realized that by the time the U.S. letters were delivered to the UN, the military operations organized to free the ship were ready to be implemented. The United States' last-minute appeal to the UN, he knew therefore, could cause criticism, rather than dispel it. The letters might be construed as a maneuver to combat subsequent charges that the U.S. failed to exhaust all diplomatic channels before taking military action. Still, he ordered the letters sent. Senator Edward Kennedy, who happened to be at the UN, agreed with the president's action, saying in the case of the *Mayaguez* he had "a unique responsibility for the protection of American lives."

At 2:30 the president shook hands with a group of Nassau County businessmen in the Roosevelt Room.

At 3:52 the National Security Council convened in the Cabinet Room. This was the fourth NSC meeting called to deal with the *Mayaguez* crisis, and as it turned out, the most crucial. The strategy of ordering simultaneous Marine assaults on Koh Tang and on the *Mayaguez* itself, supported by the bombing of selected targets on the mainland, had been formulated at the NSC meeting the night before. But the final timing and details of the operation required more discussion.

By the time this meeting began, any slight hope that China might be able to intercede with Cambodia to obtain the release of the *Mayaguez,* had been dispelled by the return of the American note. The diplomatic maneuver known as *Non Recevoir* had been used by China to indicate that it did not accept the note. But as Henry Kissinger made clear, this did not mean the Chinese had not read the note, and perhaps even attempted to act on its contents. "I am assuming Chinese Xerox machines could reproduce it in twenty-four hours," said Kissinger, who was convinced the note did reach Cambodia despite China's official hands-off policy. In returning the note in Washington and not in Peking (where U.S. Liaison Officer George Bush had interrupted a picnic to the Ming Tombs to deliver a duplicate note), Kissinger had pointed out that the Chinese were "attempting to preserve a degree of formal dissociation." He was aware that the Chinese were in the delicate position of laying themselves open to criticism by the Russians for serving as American lackeys, if they appeared to be helping the

U.S. to get the *Mayaguez* and its crew back.

One of the military options presented by the acting chairman of the Joint Chiefs of Staff at the National Security Council meeting the night before involved the use of Guam-based B-52s to strike the Cambodian mainland. The big bombers had been placed on alert. At this meeting a debate took place on whether or not to use them: Vice-President Nelson Rockefeller, Henry Kissinger, and General Scowcroft in favor; James Schlesinger, the Joint Chiefs' chairman, George Brown (who now had returned from Europe), and his deputy, General David C. Jones, against. President Ford sided with the secretary of defense and the Joint Chiefs against the use of the 52s. The fact that the aircraft carrier *Coral Sea* had overcome strong headwinds and was approaching the area off Koh Tang, was a prime consideration of the president's final decision to drop the B-52 option. Kissinger maintains that once the *Coral Sea* was known to be within striking distance, the decision against the B-52s became unanimous. Even so, the B-52s were kept gassed-up, their bomb bays loaded, and their crews on the line ready for take-off.

At 4:45 while this NSC meeting was still in progress, the president issued the orders for one Marine assault force to seize and hold Koh Tang, and for another Marine force, which was first to be placed aboard the destroyer *Holt,* to board the *Mayaguez.* At the same time he ordered U.S. aircraft to protect and support the operation. From commander in chief, the orders flowed rapidly down to the fighting men. The National Military Command Center in the Pentagon ordered Air Force Lieutenant General John J. Burns, commander of the United States Military Advisory Group in Thailand, to begin the military operation. General Burns was designated the on-the-scene commander. He in turn ordered the 56th Special Operations Wing at Utapao to launch eleven CH-53 and HH-53 helicopters with 227 Marines. (Eight helicopters with 179 Marines were directed to Koh Tang and three helicopters with 48 Marines to the *Holt* for boarding the *Mayaguez.* Also in the helicopters destined for the *Holt* were six demolition experts, six Navy civilians of the Marine Sea Command who could operate the *Mayaguez,* and one Army captain who spoke Cambodian.) The Marines, commanded by Lieutenant Colonel Randall W. Austin, commanding officer, Second Battalion, 9th Marines, part of the Third Marine Division, made final checks on the equipment and mounted their Jolly Green Giants. Austin, accompanied by staff officers and company commanders, had made a reconnaissance flight over Koh Tang and the *Mayaguez* the previous day. F-4 Phantoms and A-7 jet fighter bombers of the 388th Tactical Fighter Wing fired their engines, as did the reconnaissance jets of the 432nd Tactical Fighter Wing. The *Coral Sea* was still ninety-five nautical miles from Koh Tang, proceeding at thirty knots. She, too, launched F-4 Phantoms, A-6 Intruders, and A-7 Corsairs to soften up Koh Tang for the Marines.

The military operation was already twenty-eight minutes underway when the National Security Council meeting ended at 5:40. Calls immediately went out to Congress that the president would see the bipartisan leaders at 6:30—a signal that major action was imminent.

At 5:42 the Joint Chiefs of Staff ordered Admiral Noel Gayler, commander in chief, U.S. Pacific Forces, to initiate the supporting air strikes against three key points: a fuel storage area in the port of Kompong Som, Ream Naval Base, and Ream Airfield, where some 2,400 Cambodian troops were believed to be stationed. CINCPAC issued the orders at 6:03. Said one of Admiral Gayler's aides: "This action had a lot of *ifs* in it. It wasn't like going in and taking people out of Phnom Penh." By this time tension was high at the National Military Command Center in the Pentagon. Naval chief of operations, Admiral James Holloway III, hurried back from Boston where two Soviet warships were making the first visit to a U.S. port since World War II.

At 6:09 Secretary Kissinger popped back into the Oval Office for two minutes to discuss the *Mayaguez* in preparation for the president's briefing of congressional leaders. While the crisis demanded action by the commander in chief, the president nevertheless felt his obligations to Congress. Already some criticism had flared on Capitol Hill. Republican leaders, apparently, were pleased enough by the way the president was handling the crisis, and so were Democratic hawks, but the doves were skeptical. "There was a tremendous feeling of uneasiness," said House Majority Leader Tip O'Neill, "of where do we go from here if we don't find the crew."

The black limousines swept down from Capitol Hill through the last rush-hour traffic, bringing the bipartisan leaders to the White House. At 6:40 as the president entered the Cabinet Room to meet with the leaders, he was given a standing ovation. At the president's disposal was a map of the Gulf of Thailand and the Cambodian coast, and the usual back-up staff of State and Defense Department experts. For thirty minutes the president reviewed the crisis: the seizure of the ship, the absence of response to the notes he had sent Cambodia through the Chinese Liaison Office in Washington and the U.S. Liaison Office in Peking, and his order to prevent, if possible, the movement of boats to or from the mainland from Koh Tang, where the *Mayaguez* had been lying dead in the water for more than forty-one hours.

"We gave the Cambodians clear orders," said the president. "They disregarded them. They were not to try to take the ships from the island to the mainland." He described the small-arms fire from the gunboats and from the island. Yet, said President Ford, under the cover of darkness, the Cambodians sought to move off the island. The U.S. planes then swept in. Three boats were sunk and four were damaged, and one was permitted to proceed to the mainland.

The president did not specify, but he left the distinct impression that the pilots believed that the eighth could have contained members of the *Mayaguez* crew. The planes, he explained, did everything they could to force the boat back to the island without actually firing on it. The president then disclosed decisions taken at the National Security Council meeting which had ended barely one hour earlier: to assault the island with Marines, to put Marines aboard the *Mayaguez,* and to bomb three selected targets around Kompong Som. At the same time, the president cautioned that the surveillance specialists were not certain where most of the crew might be—hopefully either on the ship, or on the island, or in the immediate vicinity. The attack force assigned to seize the *Mayaguez,* he said, included experts to defuse any bombs that might have been rigged by the Cambodians, plus a crew to sail the ship out of there if it was still operational.

Following the briefing, President Ford invited questions from the legislators. Senator Mike Mansfield asked why he had ordered the bombing of the Kompong Som area, especially if some members of the crew were believed to be there, and the rest of them back on Koh Tang. The president conceded that some of the crew might have been onboard the boat that was permitted to reach the mainland. But he insisted that the order to bomb those specific mainland targets was necessary to prevent an attack by an estimated 2,400 Cambodian soldiers stationed around Kompong Som. Reconnaissance had also detected the presence of a number of small planes at Ream Airfield. "I am not going to risk the life of one Marine," said the president. "I'd never forgive myself." If the Cambodians attacked the Marines, he said, "It would be too great a risk not to have this supportive action on the mainland."

Senator Robert Byrd wanted assurance from the president that he would comply with the 1973 War Powers Resolution, and report to Congress within forty-eight hours of the military action he undertook in an attempt to save American lives. President Ford assured the group of his intended compliance. Senator Byrd noted that, although the War Powers Resolution did not require the president to "consult" Congress in advance of a contemplated military action, he might have—"for your own protection"— avoided any charges of overreaction if he had done so.

"As commander in chief, I have the duty," replied the president. "I acted on the basis that this was the proper exercise of my responsibilities. I believe it was the right decision. The question of doing too little weighed heavily. A counterreaction by the Cambodians would have placed the Marines' lives in jeopardy."

House Speaker Carl Albert asked the president if he couldn't have waited a bit longer before using force.

"We waited as long as we could," the president said.

James Eastland, the president pro tem of the Senate did not take active part in the discussion. He sat slumped down in his chair, mumbling several times: "Blow the hell out of 'em." Late that night to comply with the War Powers Resolution, letters to the Speaker of the House and president pro tem of the Senate, were shoved under their office doors.

Thursday, May 15

FIFTEEN

A Dissenting Vote

IT TOOK Captain Charles Theodore Miller several seconds to orient himself to his strange surroundings when he woke up at three o'clock in the morning in urgent need of a piss. First, he had to figure out who was in bed with him. Then he had to decide where they both were. Finally everything came into focus. He and Pastrano, the pantryman, were sharing a cot on the veranda at the Khmer Rouge military compound at Koh Rong Sam Lem, where the English-speaker had told everybody to sleep.

Charlie got up. He walked out on the open deck to pee over the railing. But a man in black poked him with the muzzle of his gun and motioned back to the cot. Charlie returned to the veranda, kneeled down, and peed between the bamboo slats. The guard came over and patted the cot. The message was clear. He wanted Charlie to stay in bed.

Between the buzzing of the mosquitoes and everything buzzing through his head, he never did get back to sleep. Mosquitoes were bad. Must be a lot of malaria, he thought. What in hell did LaBue, Kastl, and Conway think they were doing? Put 'em on the hot sheet. Sounded kind of stoned, laughing and hollering over in the other shack after everybody told 'em to shut up. Got grass ashore, probably. From the guy shavin' pig feed, maybe? Hell, yes, put 'em on the hot sheet and turn 'em in to Customs. You must have had fifty or sixty guys on the hot sheet one time or other.

Charlie rolled over on his back and tried to pull his shirt up over his face to ward off the mosquitoes. But he couldn't sleep that way either. Where'd the English-speaker go? Didn't sleep in one of these sheds over the water. Went down the gangway to shore. Nice kid. French educated, probably. Scared shitless of the jets. Can't think of anything else. "Sunk three gunboats," he said. "Wounded a hundred friendly Cambodian people." But he said something else: "You can all go in the morning." What did that mean? "More of their fucking lies," English said.

Charlie sat up and stretched. The guard tapped him on the shoulder to lie down. Lots of guards out there. Can't really see 'em. Just their shadows slinkin' up and down the boardwalks and over on the shore. Khmer Rouge, great for chopping heads. Read about the bloodbath in Phnom Penh. Nobody could prove it. Just a rumor in the papers. If I have to meet my maker, hope they shoot me. Faster that way. Why worry? You got sixty-two years of your life spent already. Annie and me, we've become kind of a religious family together. Go to church on holy days. Saturday nights, too, usually five o'clock mass. But I've got a few bucks in the bank she could live on. Took me down to the safe deposit box one day and showed me this envelope. "What's in it?" I asked. "Open it," she said. There was thirty-three thousand bucks she'd been puttin' away. And all those twenty-dollar Balboas. Biggest coins in the world. That's why all the sailors bought 'em. Worth two hundred bucks apiece today.

The first light streaked the sky. "Everybody up," shouted Charlie. He wanted to be ready. Over on the shore he'd seen a barrel of water. Since it wasn't pitch black outside anymore, he figured the guards would let them walk over. "Come on, everybody. Get up. You only have half an hour to brush your teeth and wash your face."

They all walked across the gangplank to where the barrel was. Charlie watched the chief brush his teeth with his finger. "One of the guards has been trying to steal my flashlight and I wouldn't let him take it," said Harrington.

Actually, Harrington had slept pretty well. Burt Coombes had loaned him his cot for a couple of hours, but he couldn't wake the chief to get it back. When Harrington finally woke up and saw Burt stretched out down on the floor he thought, well, I've slept under worse conditions even when I was paying for it. Like the night in Baltimore on the old *President Cleveland* when he and Engine Department Yeoman Johnny Blake, and the water tender Rod Blanchette, splurged and took a sixty-eight–dollar suite in the Southern Hotel. That was a lot of money in those days, especially since nobody got to sleep in the suite. Rod Blanchette shacked up with some girl in the suburbs. Johnny Blake spent the night in jail. And Harrington got drunk and slept in a snowbank in the back of the hotel.

The water in the barrel didn't look too bad, so Charlie dipped his finger in and rubbed it across his teeth like the chief. When he looked up the English-speaker was standing beside him. "Good morning, Captain Miller," he said politely. The compound commander was with him, stripped to the waist. His muscles rippled as he scooped a cup of water out of the barrel. Yesterday Charlie hadn't noticed how strong and sinewy the compound commander was.

"At six o'clock," said the English-speaker, "we will talk to the first commander in Kompong Som. We will ask him if the high commander in Phnom Penh has given approval for you and your crew to leave."

Charlie looked at the lean, clean-cut Cambodian, a little taller than he was and less than half his age. Is he tricking us? Charlie wondered. Keeping our hopes alive while his Khmer Rouge superiors decide on their revenge for the hundred friendly Cambodians killed or maimed? "Last night I thought you said we could go," Charlie said.

"Yes. But first we must call," said the English-speaker. This morning, laying there on the cot next to Pastrano, Charlie had decided to keep everybody informed, even if the news turned out to be bad. Otherwise they'd sit around and stew. "Looks like we're going to have to wait, fellas," he said.

"What'd I tell you, Captain," said English, shaking his shaggy red hair. "More goddamn lies." Then he walked away. Charlie was grateful that English didn't blow up. But Friedler, LaBue, and Jack Mullis, the bosun, picked it up from English and started muttering: "It's a bunch of bullshit, Captain. They're just stringing you along. We're not going back to the ship." LaBue made a move to address the English-speaker himself. Charlie cut him off.

"I'm the captain," he said. "You're under my command, whether you're on the ship or on shore. We're just going to wait until these fellows hear from Phnom Penh."

Charlie watched a chicken with her baby chicks prance by. They reminded him of the time his father quit his job in a North Chicago coal yard and went into the chicken business in Arlington, Illinois. It was when his father was still married to the "Heil Hitler Mrs. Schultz." Charlie's father would buy 500 baby chicks and 500 baby ducks at a time. Once, Charlie remembered, he had 5,000 baby ducks and 10,000 baby chicks. But Mrs. Schultz got mad and went back to work as a hotel maid in Chicago. Charlie's father chased after her, leaving Charlie and his sister alone for a week with all the chickens and ducks. It was January and he and his sister had to fire up a boiler each night to keep the chickens and ducks from freezing to death. But one night 500 or 600 piled up in a corner and smothered. The neighbors reported it to the police. They arrested Charlie's father and threw him in jail and sent Charlie and his sister off to juvenile hall in Chicago. That was how he became an orphan.

At ten minutes after six the English-speaker and the compound commander took Charlie and the chief back to their room while they called Kompong Som on the U.S. Army fieldpack radio. First the English-speaker talked to Kompong Som, then he talked to the compound commander, then the compound commander talked to

Kompong Som. Charlie watched the cords in the compound commander's neck tighten and untighten as he talked, trying to get some clue how the conversation was progressing. The spasms were contagious. He could feel the muscles in his stomach grabbing and letting go. The English-speaker smiled. Maybe everything's all right, Charlie decided. Maybe they're going to let us go.

"They are still waiting in Kompong Som," the English-speaker said. "The high commander in Phnom Penh has not given them permission to release the crew." Charlie detected genuine regret in the English-speaker's voice. But the chief, he saw, was getting red in the face under all his mosquito bites. He must have slept pretty hard not to have felt those hummingbird-sized mosquitoes, Charlie thought. On me the mosquitoes kept practicing landings and take-offs, and refueling their tanks all night long.

"Here comes the old stall," Harrington whispered.

But at 6:30 the walkie-talkie blared with an incoming call. The English-speaker caught it and the conversation terminated in ten seconds. "Yes," he said, "the high commander says you and your men can go back to the ship." Calling off the American planes had taken on a high priority in Phnom Penh, Charlie was certain. For some reason he felt no surge of elation.

"Can we go now?" asked Charlie.

"Yes," said the English-speaker, "but first we must prepare the manifests."

Cargo manifests? Charlie wondered. He had mentioned the ship's manifest to the English-speaker yesterday. But they were in his file cabinet on the ship. "What kind of manifests?" he asked.

"I will tell you what they are, and you can write them down," explained the English-speaker.

Charlie patted the breast pocket of his shirt. His ballpoint pen was still clipped inside next to his eyeglass case. But he had no paper. Vern Greenlin, the first engineer, had a notebook, he remembered. He had seen him writing in it. "I'm keeping a diary for the Downieville *Mountain Messenger,*" Greenlin had told him.

"Chief," said Charlie turning to Harrington. "Go get the first's notebook."

"Don't forget, you better get their names, Charlie," Harrington said. "We better find out who we're dealing with in case there are any repercussions." Harrington somehow had the notion they all might get involved in some big investigation when they got back to the States. He had already mentioned this possibility to Charlie.

Charlie sat on the English-speaker's cot with the small spiral-bound notebook in his lap. He put on his glasses. Half the crew clustered around the cot, curious to find out what was going on.

"What is your name?" asked Charlie.

The English-speaker nodded at his muscular superior. "The compound commander who is also the second commander in Kompong Som, is named Chhan," he said. He took Charlie's ballpoint and printed: SECOND COMMANDER—CHHAN. "I am the speaker. My name is "Samkol." He printed the word SPEAKER, and beside it, SAMKOL.

Then he commenced dictating. "Manifest number one," he started out. But he stopped. Like many a young executive facing an old stenographer with pen poised expectantly on the other side of the desk, the English-speaker choked up. His fluency suddenly failed him. "Four ships destroyed and one hundred friendly people wounded," he blurted in staccato little sentences.

Where did the fourth ship come from, Charlie wondered? Another gunboat must have been sunk during the night.

"Manifest number two," continued the English-speaker, "Cambodian people treat the crew very good and no harm was done to the crew of forty people." A little gas and shrapnel, Charlie thought. But we can hardly blame the Cambodians for them. Charlie glanced at his watch: 6:45. He worried about the delay. But the English-speaker charged ahead. He now seemed to have the manifests firmly fixed in his mind.

"Manifest number three," he said. But another fuse blew in the

Cambodian's English-speaking circuitry. "The crew respect the country of Cambodia and the forty crew are responsible for the people and no more damage to the country—no bombs shooting, no airplanes fly over Cambodia." Charlie stared at his notebook and tried to untangle the sentence. If I understand that one correctly, he thought, Cambodia is going to hold the *Mayaguez* crew personally responsible for any further death and destruction done to this country by the American jets. He might have objected, but he didn't. There wasn't time.

"Manifest number four," continued the English-speaker, "The Cambodian high commander has contacted the International and the forty crew about the numbers one, two, three point same as written. The International knows the situation very bad for country Cambodia." International? wondered Charlie. What kind of International? Maybe the UN, or the Communist International? Or maybe he's just stalling around waiting for another call on the walkie-talkie from Kompong Som.

"Manifest number five," said the English-speaker smiling, "Forty crew very friendly to people of Cambodia. Good friends." That may be a slight exaggeration, Charlie thought. Anyway, he sensed the Cambodian was finally running down.

"Manifest number six. The people of Cambodia no like war and want peace and want many friend in the International and have forty friend in this crew." The English-speaker flashed his polite smile. "That is all, Captain Miller," he said. "Please sign."

Charlie did as the English-speaker instructed. At the bottom of the last page he wrote: "C.T. Miller, for the forty crew." What use can they possibly have for a document like this in Cambodia? he wondered. The English-speaker reached over and picked Charlie's ballpoint pen off the cot. In large block letters under Charlie's signature he wrote: THE PEOPLE CAMBODIA GOOD FRIENDLY WITH 40 PEOPLES U.S. Then he handed the signed document back to Charlie.

"Captain Miller," he said, "you keep it."

Charlie didn't understand. "You want me to take it back to the ship with me?" he asked. "I thought this signed statement was for you and for Cambodia."

"No, it is for you," insisted the Cambodian. He looked hurt, as if Charlie was spurning this written expression of friendship which he had intended as his parting gift.

"Oh, fine," said Charlie. "I will bring this back to the ship." But he still didn't understand. The Cambodian had insisted on his signing what amounted to a receipt for the release of the forty American prisoners. Now he was giving Charlie back his receipt. How's this young fella going to know if I crumple up this six-point manifesto of his and toss it in the ocean? he wondered.

"Can we go now?" Charlie asked.

"After you vote," said the English-speaker.

"Vote?" said Charlie. Once again he didn't understand. Up till now there had been no communication breakdowns between him and the Cambodian. Not one since the English-speaker first stuck out his hand and said: "Welcome to Cambodia." Suddenly we're talking two different languages, Charlie thought. "Who gets to vote?" he asked. "And what are we voting for?"

"The forty crew must vote," said the English-speaker. "Isn't that the way you do things in your democracy? The manifests must be unanimous."

"OK," said Charlie, "I'll take a vote." He stepped into the center of the big veranda. "All right, fellas," he said, "we're going to take a vote." The crew, he noticed, was beginning to look a little raggedy—mosquito-bitten and unshaven and dirty, in the same sweaty clothes for two days and nights.

"Let's get the fuck outa here, Cap," he heard a voice call.

Charlie glanced at his watch: 7:03. The sun was well up in the sky. The jets would be out there now. Better hurry, he thought. "Fellas, I'm going to read six points which the English-speaker here has asked me to write down." He pointed to the young Cambodian whose name he had just learned was Samkol. "Then if you agree to these six points unanimously, we're going to go."

He put his glasses back on. The tortoise-shell tops and rimless bottoms made him look more corner druggist than sea captain. Holding Vern Greenlin's spiral notebook, also containing the diary for the Downieville *Mountain Messenger,* Charlie started reading. When he came to the end of manifest number six, he looked up and said: "All those in favor say aye."

A chorus of "ayes," "yeas," and "yups" rang out. Charlie glanced over at the English-speaker and the compound commander to make certain they were both satisfied.

"I'm not signing that confession," he heard somebody call out. Charlie wheeled around. The minutes were slipping by, and here's this shit-disturber in his own crew. It was AB Tom LaBue.

"The captain's not asking *you* to sign anything, LaBue," snapped Cliff Harrington. For the past ten minutes while Charlie had been writing out the manifests, Harrington had been running down a mental checklist of things he would do to start up the plant fast. "All he's asking *you* to do is agree to the six points. The captain signed them."

LaBue stepped forward to face Harrington. A short and stocky sailor with dark hair, he had sailed out of San Francisco on the *Mayaguez* on October 12, 1974. "I don't want the captain signing a confession for me," he said.

Harrington blew up. "Wait a minute, LaBue," he said. "Where the hell do you get confession out of this?"

"What do you call this?" yelled LaBue. "It's a confession. And it's against my principles. I don't want the captain signing that thing for me."

Charlie glanced over at the English-speaker. His thin, sensitive face was knotted into a frown, as he strained to catch the American slang words being hurled back and forth. The muscle-bound compound commander stood next to him scowling. Charlie turned back to LaBue. The AB now had his two feet planted firmly apart, facing Harrington like a welterweight coming in for round two.

Before LaBue could say anything, Harrington let him have it again.

"Where do you see the word confession, LaBue? And even if it is a confession, LaBue, we're living in a democratic society, aren't we? The vote was thirty-nine to one."

That didn't satisfy LaBue. "I've got my rights," he shouted. "I've got the right to speak up."

Charlie suddenly remembered that there had been trouble with LaBue once before. Six or seven weeks earlier the chief mate had received an anonymous handwritten letter from a member of the deck department complaining about not making enough overtime. "When I don't get overtime I get mad," the letter said. "When I get mad I get pissed. And when I get pissed I get dangerous." Charlie didn't take the letter seriously. But it was the kind of threat you couldn't just ignore. Not on a ship with everybody living in such close quarters. He and the chief mate had compared the handwriting of the note with all the signatures on the draw. La-Bue's matched perfectly. LaBue had finally admitted writing it. Before Harrington could respond, Charlie waded in.

"LaBue, the best thing for you to do is keep quiet," he said. "Just shut up and we'll all go back to the ship."

Charlie turned back to the English-speaker, whose expression now had changed from dismay to anger, as if the heat of the argument was directed at him personally. Maybe we're not going back to the ship after all, Charlie thought. "This is only one man talking," he said to the Cambodian. "There are thirty-nine others who don't think I'm signing a confession."

"Man, you got the right to speak up. But this isn't the time," said Tyrone Matthews quietly to LaBue. He was standing right behind him.

"Keep out of it, LaBue," yelled Gerald Bayless. Suddenly the rest of the crew erupted: "Shut up, LaBue. Sit down, LaBue. Fuck you, LaBue," they shouted.

"Everybody shut up," yelled Charlie. He pointed to the English-speaker and the compound commander. "All these two men want is for the world to know that Cambodia was friendly to us. All this paper says is they treated us right, and we were friendly to them. It's no confession."

"LaBue," Charlie Miller said, eying the AB sternly. "You can't be right, because then all the rest of the crew is wrong. The best thing for you is to shut up."

AB Tom LaBue shut up.

Charlie suddenly found himself jammed between the English-speaker and the compound commander, with his arms around both of them, while an armed guard laid down his AK-47 and took the picture. Charlie never did see where the brand-new Canon F-10 camera came from.

"Now we will go eat breakfast," the English-speaker said.

"This crew don't ever eat breakfast," Charlie replied. He just couldn't stand one more delay.

SIXTEEN

Assaults on Land and Sea

COMMANDER ROBERT A. PETERSON sized up the problem facing him precisely at 7:20 A.M. on the fifteenth day of May, 1975. It wasn't the most monumental problem he had faced in nineteen years in the Navy. Nevertheless it was nettlesome. He had to snuggle his ship, the U.S.S. *Harold E. Holt,* up against another ship which had just been doused with tear gas and probably still had lurking aboard her an untold number of men armed with automatic weapons. In fact, just thirty minutes earlier, studying this ship through binoculars, six armed Cambodians had been observed standing on the deck. They were a mixed bag. Two wore black shirts, two wore blue, and two white. But their guns were clearly visible.

Now as he approached the *Mayaguez,* Bob Peterson had to make an important decision. Because the *Holt* was a Knox class destroyer with a single engine and one propeller, it would be much easier for him to put the port side of the *Holt* up against the starboard side of the *Mayaguez.* Then when he reversed his engine, the *Holt* would back to port. But this morning there were other factors. Was the *Mayaguez* swinging fast at anchor? Which way was the wind blowing the tear gas? Did he want to put the *Holt* between *Mayaguez* and the island, not knowing what capability they had on the beach to shoot at him. Over on the beach, more than an hour ago, he had seen the A-65s and A-7s diving on the island, softening it up for the Marines. But since the Marines had gone in, he had heard a lot of gunfire and some loud explosions coming from the beach. He had also seen the pillars of black smoke where a couple of the helos had crashed.

At the last minute Peterson decided to go to the port side of the *Mayaguez* and shield himself from the island. He pulled his gas mask down over his face. Between his contact lenses and the goggles of the gas mask, it was hard to see. He peered over at the white superstructure of the *Mayaguez*. His eyes jumped from deck to deck looking for the armed men. Then his eyes probed the shadowy spaces between the silver containers. All he could see were lingering patches of white smoke, laid down by the low-flying jets when they engulfed the ship in tear gas ten minutes ago. No life over there, he thought. But then he couldn't see inside where the men would be hiding.

He inched the *Holt* closer. Ordinarily coming alongside a pier or another ship, he'd stand off a ways and throw heaving lines across. Then he'd winch the ship in. But on the *Mayaguez* there was nobody to catch his lines. He had fenders over the side. They would cushion the blow. Still, it would be hard to snuggle the *Holt* up against the *Mayaguez* without stoving in one or the other hull. And once he got the *Holt* safely up against the container ship, he'd have to hold her steady while the Marines scrambled over and grabbed his lines. But the Marines, they'll have other things to worry about, Peterson thought.

He looked down at the Marines. Their fifty-calibre machine guns were trained on the *Mayaguez*, ready to rake her with fire. The assault group was also ready to go: crouched down with gas masks on, the muzzles of their M-16s pointed at the container ship. The forty-eight Marines had arrived at six o'clock. At least they started coming at six. Took them twenty minutes to climb down the rope ladders out of the three helos. Six demolition experts had come with them to check for booby traps and bombs. Six Marine Sea Command personnel to start up the plant on the *Mayaguez*, and one Cambodian-speaking Army captain had come too.

He moved the *Holt* closer. Only twenty feet of water separated the two hulls now. Peterson studied the freeboard of the two ships. Almost a perfect match. The main deck of the *Holt* lined up beautifully with the main deck of the *Mayaguez*. It would be easy for the Marines. They could just jump across. That was just one of his missions, putting the Marines aboard. His other mission was to rig some kind of a bridle, cut the anchor chain and tow the *Mayaguez* away. He'd be glad when the action started. His ship had been the first to arrive. Since midnight they had been waiting for the others. Now the *Vega* and *Wilson* were there too. The *Coral Sea* with all her escorts: *Gridley, Bausell, Lang,* and *Mispillion,* were two hours away. The *Coral Sea,* of course, was already in the action. She had launched her planes at dawn. "Don't rush," Bob Peterson cautioned himself. "In one more minute the action could start for you."

He glanced down again at the Marines. Young kids. They looked tense, crouching low as if they expected to draw fire any second from the *Mayaguez*. They'll probably forget our lines, he thought. He cupped his hands to his mouth. "Hey, you guys. Don't forget our lines," he shouted.

He looked down at the narrow sliver of green water between the two ships. The rope fenders were about to be squashed flat between the grey and the black hull. The hulls kissed. I must be living right today, he thought.

"Marines over the side!" he shouted. The Marines seemed to hesitate. "Marines over the side!" he shouted again. It's a strange sight, Bob Peterson thought, seeing a bunch of young Marines storm a beat-up old cargo ship like that.

When Robert A. Peterson was ten years old and growing up in Emmett, Idaho, the ship he was now looking at was already getting her baptism of fire. *White Falcon* was her name, and *Fleetwing, Fairwind, Flying Eagle,* and *White Squall* were some of her sisters, since many ships of her particular class (C-2-AJ1) started their seagoing lives as Indians. Unfortunately her war record was not precisely kept. And many of the men who sailed her in World War II no longer survive. But a few of the facts are known. On May 14, 1944, thirty-one years ago to the day (taking into account the international dateline), the *White Falcon* sailed out of New York harbor on her maiden voyage under the command of Captain J. Walsh. On her first trip she eluded U-boats and reached Loch Ewe, Scotland, in time to deliver 5,080 tons of Army cargo for the Normandy invasion, although she herself safely sat out D-day in South Shields, Scotland. She was wounded once during the war (though it is no longer known whether by torpedo or storm) in the North Sea, somewhere between Solent and Le Havre. Part of her cargo was damaged and it took sixteen days to get her shipshape again. She also made wartime voyages into the Mediterranean to Marseilles, Naples, Barry, and Oran. But on V-E Day she was back in convoy on the North Atlantic, five days out of New York bound for Antwerp, carrying her last combat load for World War II.

After World War II, *White Falcon* found herself mixed up in tribal wars in British and Portuguese East Africa, in places like Mombasa, Dar es Salaam, Tanga, and Lourenço Marques, and in banana republic revolutions in Central and South America. *White Falcon,* still bearing her Indian name and wearing her grey war paint, covered most of the ports of the western world from *A* (Antofogasta) to *Z* (Zanzibar), carrying everything from thirty-calibre bullets to tanks in war, and from matchbooks to windmills in peace. Now, as an old lady in black, and bearing her fourth name, she was being boarded by forty-eight American fighting men from D Company, First Battalion, Fourth Marines, under the command of thirty-eight-year-old Major Ray E. Porter of Mountainaire, New Mexico.

At 7:28 A.M. the Marines swarmed over onto the main deck of the *Mayaguez.* Twelve of them scaled the outside ladders to the bridge, their M-16s held at the ready. The rest fanned out over the ship. They moved cautiously through the tear gas trapped in the bilious green companionways, threw open cabin doors, checked the galley, the officers' saloon, and then cautiously descended the steep ladders into the engineroom. Nobody was there. The *Mayaguez* had been abandoned. The six armed Cambodians who had been observed through binoculars forty minutes earlier, either had a small boat tied to the starboard side out of sight of the approaching *Holt,* or they swam away. No boat was seen pulling away from the *Mayaguez.* There was only one sign of life. The Marines claim they found warm bowls of rice and cups of warm tea. But since the power was off on the *Mayaguez,* the Cambodians either brought their own cookstoves, or that morning was already hot enough to make the bowls and cups warm to the touch.

At 8:30 Major Porter and Captain Walt Wood raised the American flag over the recaptured ship. Since the retaking of Iwo Jima the Marines have been good at recording their historic flag-raisings. The retaking of the *Mayaguez* was no exception. A photographer was on hand to snap the moment. But strangely, the *Mayaguez* had been flying no American flag when the Cambodians seized her. She hardly ever did fly a flag in that part of the world. The wind on the South China Sea ripped them to pieces.

The guided missile destroyer *Wilson* charged onto the battle scene at Koh Tang at 7 A.M. with her four boilers on line, her general-quarters horns hooting, and her five-inch guns trained on the beach where the action was already in full swing. Commander J. Michael Rodgers with his *Henry B. Wilson* baseball cap pulled down over his pale, pudgy face, was on the bridge. He approached the situation at hand with the same clinical precision he would apply to one of his two-move chess problems. As usual, the night before, when his ship was still plowing through the seas at thirty-one knots trying to keep its appointment at Koh Tang, he had sat in his cabin pitting his skill against the toughest two-move situations the chess masters could conjure up.

Now standing on the bridge he surveyed the battle scene. Well, the *Holt* is on the northwest side of the island, he reasoned. I'll come in from the southeast. Then if there are any heavy gun emplacements on the beach, they'll have to divide their fire.

These were familiar waters for Mike Rodgers. Waiting for the evacuation of Phnom Penh, his ship had been kept on station a few miles south of Kompong Som for more than three weeks in March and April. At that time, of course, he had not ventured in close to the Wai or Tang Islands, though the Khmer Rouge didn't finally occupy them until at least a week after they took over the capital on April 17.

As the *Wilson* came around the northeastern tip of Koh Tang he studied the action. There were plenty of aircraft—Corsairs, Phantoms, and Intruders, he could see—supporting the Marines ashore. A mile off the beach he could still hear the heavy exchange of gunfire: the pop and crack of small arms interspersed with the soft whoomp of mortars. The tattoo of machine guns drifted across the water too. With his binoculars he tried to pick out the friendly lines, but he couldn't. He could just make out the top of one helo sitting in the water, where it had been shot down. A black column of smoke marked another helo burning on the beach. He could also see the pilot house of a Cambodian gunboat sticking out of the water near the beach. There was an abundance of targets for the *Henry B. Wilson*'s two five-inch guns. But so far he had neither requested permission nor been asked by the airborne command post to fire. For the moment, at least, Rodgers and the *Wilson* were just sort of monitoring the war which had commenced less than one hour ago. All of the *Wilson*'s radars were being manned. They scanned the sky for any sign of hostile aircraft. American-supplied T-28s were all Cambodia had. But not even these appeared. So far all the fire had come from the ground, the hottest spot appearing to be the tree line about seventy-five yards in back of the beach.

The crescent-shaped beach, which started near the northeastern tip of the island, curved gently around to the base of Koh Tang's lone hill rising above the northwest promontory. Mike

Rodgers's binoculars swept along the curve of the beach. He was trying to see if he could spot Cambodian gun emplacements, when the lookout called back that he saw a head in the water off the port bow. The *Wilson* was running about a mile offshore. Rodgers turned his ship and steamed towards the head. Suddenly he saw red smoke coming from the water and spotted a second head. Then he saw quite a few heads. They were being swept out from shore by the current. He stopped the ship. A gun emplacement on the shore started peppering away at the *Wilson,* which had become a fat stationary target with a serious rescue mission on its hands. Rodgers ignored the gunfire from the beach and lowered the gig, generally used to carry him, as the ship's captain, and the commodore to shore wherever the *Wilson* was peacefully at anchor. The gig had two M-60 machine guns on it, and this morning they were manned by Petty Officers First Class Alvin Ellis and Thomas Noble, as the gig set about plucking all the Marines and Air Force helicopter crew members it could find, out of the water. When the gig returned, it had thirteen burned, wounded, and half-drowned passengers aboard. Their CH-53 had been shot down twenty yards off the beach. The other thirteen men aboard—ten Marines, two Navy men, and one airman—had been killed. One Marine on the beach had already been killed by a Claymore mine. The KIAs of Koh Tang's one-hour-old war already stood at fourteen. The *Henry B. Wilson* turned her bow towards the *Mayaguez* to see if she needed assistance.

SEVENTEEN

First Word from Phnom Penh

PRESIDENT FORD RETURNED to the Oval Office at 7:47 P.M. from his briefing of the bipartisan leaders of Congress. He felt drained. It had been a demanding one hour and five minutes, the president himself delivering a thirty-minute summary of events leading up to the ordered Marine assaults on Koh Tang and the *Mayaguez.* Then for the final thirty-five minutes he had answered the legislators' questions. The session, he felt, had gone well. The standing ovation at the beginning had pleased him. And at the end he came away believing the leaders were—if not solidly—well behind him. Before he left the Cabinet Room, General Brent Scowcroft had advised him that the 48-man Marine unit had already been placed aboard the destroyer escort *Holt,* starting at 6:58 P.M. Washington time, and that the first elements of the 179-man Marine reinforced rifle company had landed on Koh Tang at 7:20 P.M. General Scowcroft and Senator John Stennis, chairman of the Armed Services Committee, accompanied the president back to the Oval Office. The president remained for only two minutes. Then he walked back to the residence to shower and put on his tuxedo for the working dinner which had been scheduled for 8 P.M. with Premier Joop M. den Uyl of the Netherlands. The president and premier had yet to complete the arrangements for Ford's forthcoming meeting with the NATO leaders in Brussels. The president sent word that he would be late, and dinner would be delayed until 8:30.

At 8:15 Henry Kissinger was in the middle of a shower at the

White House, preparing also to attend the black-tie dinner for the Dutch premier, when he was delivered a summary of a broadcast from Phnom Penh by the R.G.N.U.C., or Royal Government of National Union of Cambodia, as the Khmer Rouge now call themselves. The nineteen-minute broadcast had been monitored in Bangkok by FBIS, the Foreign Broadcast Information Service, an independent U.S. government agency funded by the CIA. The broadcast had commenced at 7:07 P.M. Washington time. It was 8:06 before a translation had been rushed to completion and put on the FBIS wire. This was the first communication of any sort, public or private, which the U.S. had received from Cambodia in connection with the capture of the *Mayaguez.*

The secretary of state was still toweling himself as he read over a brief and partially garbled version of the broadcast. The full transcript, not obtained until later, turned out to be a long and repetitious propaganda tirade by Cambodia's new information minister, Hu Nim. It accused the United States of continuing and systematic spying on Cambodia since the Communists had taken control on April 17, charging that: "In the air U.S. imperialist planes have been conducting daily espionage flights over Cambodia. On the ground U.S. imperialism has planted its strategic forces to conduct subversive sabotage and destruction activities in the various cities. On the sea U.S. imperialist spy ships have entered Cambodia's territorial waters and engaged in espionage activities there almost daily."

The broadcast then went on to cite individual Thai fishing boats which it claimed were manned by admitted CIA agents who came ashore armed with plastic bombs and shortwave radios to destroy Cambodia's ports, factories, and strategic military positions.

The broadcast ran on for eight minutes before it mentioned the *Mayaguez.* It first described the apprehension and detention on May 7 of a Panamanian ship, which the broadcast claimed, had among its crew, Americans. "But on May 12 at 1400," the broadcast stated, "our patrol cited another large vessel steaming toward our waters. We took no action at first. The ship continued to intrude deeper into our waters passing the Wai Islands eastward to a point four or five kilometers beyond the islands. Seeing that the ship intentionally violated our waters, our patrol then stopped it in order to examine and question it and report back to higher authorities. This vessel sails in the form of a merchant ship code-named *Mayaguez*, flying American flags and manned by an American crew.

"While they were questioning the ship, two American F-105 aircrafts kept circling over the ship and over the Wai and Tang Islands and Sihanoukville port area. At 0530, May 14, six U.S. F-105 and F-111 aircraft resumed taking turns strafing and bombing. According to a preliminary report, two of our patrol vessels were sunk. We still have no precise idea of the extent of the damage done, or the number killed among our patrolmen and the American crewmen."

The broadcast proceeded to call these military actions, "savage, barbarous acts of imperialism," which "the Ford administration must bear full responsibility for." The broadcast also charged that "the ship came to violate our waters, conduct espionage, and provoke incidents to create pretexts or mislead the opinion of the world's people, the American people, and the American politicians, pretending that the Cambodian nation and people are the provocateurs while feining innocence on their part.

"We are confident that the world's people as well as the American people, youth, and politicians who love peace and justice will clearly see that the Cambodian people—a small, poor, and needy people just emerging from the U.S. imperialist war of aggression—have no intention and no wherewithal, no possibility of capturing an American ship cruising the open seas at large. We were able to capture it only because it had violated our territorial waters too flagrantly, and had come too close to our nose.

"The charge leveled by the U.S. imperialists—that we are sea pirates—is too much," the broadcast stated.

Information Minister Hu Nim saved the big news for the very end of the broadcast. "Regarding the *Mayaguez* ship," he said, "we have no intention of detaining it permanently and we have no desire to stage provocations. We only want to know the reason for its coming and to warn it against violating our waters again.

"Wishing to provoke no one or to make trouble, adhering to the stand of peace and neutrality, we will release the ship, but we will not allow the U.S. imperialists to violate our territorial waters, conduct espionage in our territorial waters, provoke incidents in our territorial waters, or force us to release their ships whenever they want, by applying threats."

The broadcast did not mention what Cambodia was planning to do with Captain Charles T. Miller and his crew, alluding only to the possibility that some of them might have been killed by the U.S. planes. Kissinger had only a one-page summary of the broadcast at this moment. Since the broadcast made no mention of the crew, the secretary of state was determined, even after he read the summary, to keep pressure on the Cambodian authorities. He still feared they might move the ship or the crew, as he said later: "We did not know whether the men were on the ship, Koh Tang, or the mainland."

At 8:23 President Ford finished putting on his tuxedo and went to the Red Room for a fast before-dinner drink with Premier den Uyl of the Netherlands. The president was enjoying the first sips of his martini-on-the-rocks at 8:29 when Kissinger called about the broadcast. Kissinger conveyed the points covered by the one-page summary, and the two men discussed Cambodia's announced intention to release the ship. It was academic. Precisely one minute before Kissinger called, the first U.S. Marines had hopped across from the U.S.S. *Holt* to the deck of the *Mayaguez,* and were in the process of retaking the ship. The Marines did not know yet that the ship had been abandoned.

In recalling the moment of his telephone call from Kissinger, the president said: "The secretary told me that the word had come that they were releasing the ship. And I said to the secretary, 'They don't mention the crew,' and apparently in the information Henry had, he had not been told or the announcement didn't include the crew. So I said to him, 'Proceed as we had agreed, with the air strikes and the full operation.' "

Over the phone Kissinger and the president agreed that Ford should nevertheless respond immediately, acknowledging that he was aware of the broadcast, and promising to call off all military operations as soon as the crew was released. The problem was how to get the president's response to Phnom Penh quickly. It was decided that the only possible way was through the press. The conversation with Kissinger lasted eight minutes. While the president rejoined his guests in the Red Room, Kissinger called Press Secretary Ron Nessen. "We've got to use you to get a message to the Cambodians," said the secretary excitedly. "They've got to read it on AP." (It has been suggested that Kissinger might have meant AFP—Agence France Presse).

At 8:41 the president and his Dutch guests proceeded to the State Dining Room. Meanwhile, downstairs in the White House Press Room, Ron Nessen read a statement addressed to the Cambodian government: "As you know we have seized the ship," Nessen said. "As soon as you issue a statement that you are prepared to release the crew members that you hold, unconditionally and immediately, we will promptly cease military operations."

Nessen then said to the newsmen: "Go file."

EIGHTEEN

"Are You the Crew of the Mayaguez?*"*

AT 7:29 A.M., the very minute United States Marines were seizing his ship, and Gerald Ford was being informed by Henry Kissinger of Phnom Penh's intent to release it anyway, the captain and crew of the *Mayaguez* were setting out in a fishing boat from the Cambodian shore—a fact which would have amazed the president, the secretary of state, and all the Marines fighting and dying on Koh Tang.

The fishing boat's name was *Sinvari,* a fact Charlie Miller didn't know. He knew only that it was the same boat which had delivered them yesterday through rockets and gas, first to Kompong Som, and finally to the military compound at Koh Rong Sam Lem. Since yesterday he had learned, however, that the fishing boat was Thai, not Cambodian, and that its five-man crew were prisoners like himself. Only they had been prisoners for five months, and might remain so for many more.

Charlie looked back. The hodge-podge of bamboo sheds standing in the water on their skinny teakwood legs, were receding. But the English-speaker, a small figure in black, kept on waving. Charlie felt drained. Were they getting away this time? Or would they be called back again? Or the jets, out there screeching and screaming and scaring the piss out of the Cambodians, would they pounce on this fishing boat and blow it to bits? Well, the way things were going this morning, they probably would.

"Say, Charlie, you know what the definition of a shit-disturber is?" said the chief. "Well, everybody's down in hell standing up to their nose in shit, when this new guy comes down and starts telling all the old hands how terrible it is. 'Wait till the Shriners come by in their motorboats,' they all yell."

Harrington, Charlie could tell, was elated. His angry face-off with LaBue hadn't spoiled the prospects of being free. Actually, LaBue wasn't bad. A hard worker. And he'd come and apologized when they got on the boat.

The second fishing boat, the one with most of the guards on, was right behind them now. "Jesus, tell them not to shoot if the jets come," Charlie had warned the English-speaker back on the dock. "If they shoot, the jets will shoot back."

"And you will contact the American government when you get on your ship," the English-speaker had pleaded. "Tell them to stop the jets."

They had pulled away from the dock at 7:20. But then the boat had turned around and gone back. They had forgotten some of the guards.

"We're off and running now," Charlie said to Cliff Harrington. The two boats were running northeast to get out of the beautiful emerald bay. Then they turned right around the rocky promontory forming the front paws of the kitten-shaped island. Charlie scanned the light overcast for jets. They were out in the open sea now. The sky was as empty as the sea.

"Twenty-four–mile straight shot to the ship," Charlie said as they drew abeam of the stone lighthouse on the southern tip of Koh Rong Sam Lem. Harrington didn't reply. He was listening to the slap of the sea against their bow.

"Now what?" said Harrington.

Charlie hadn't noticed the other fishing boat pulling up on the port side. The Cambodian ensign was waving for them to stop.

Mysteriously, he had shown up on the dock this morning. Charlie had figured he was probably back on the *Mayaguez* or perhaps on Koh Tang. But there he was, down on the dock, all smiles.

He wasn't smiling now. He was motioning frantically for the captain of the Thai fishing boat to stop. "What the hell's this. They turn us loose, then they grab us again," Harrington said. "Never pays to get too confident," he said. "That's what I always say." Harrington liked to tell the story about the *Panama*. They were coming into the dock in San Francisco. Harrington, of course, was down in the engineroom and didn't see it happen. But all of a sudden there was a sickening crash. He figured they must have hit a ferry and he immediately worried that a lot of people might have been killed. Then he decided it couldn't be too bad because they were still going half-ahead. When he came topside he discovered that a dense fog had suddenly enveloped the forward half of the *Panama,* even though the captain and the pilot were standing in bright sunshine back on the bridge. The *Panama* plowed eighty-five feet into a new pier. But the captain still didn't know what happened and he dropped anchor right on the dock. They ran the picture in all the papers. "Even if skies are sunny, don't get too confident," Harrington always said.

The other fishing boat pulled right alongside until the two boats were gunwhale-to-gunwhale. Then the Cambodian ensign hopped across into the Thai boat. "He must have got a call on his walkie-talkie," Charlie said. He had seen the Cambodian ensign bring his walkie-talkie with him into the wheelhouse of the other boat. "Maybe the jets are out by the island." That was a thought which had been gnawing at Charlie all morning.

Suddenly the captain of their fishing boat started jumping up and down and shouting in Thai. Then he shouted in English. "We free. We free," he yelled. The four other fishermen were jumping up and down too. Charlie watched all of the armed guards in their boat step across into the other boat. Then the ensign stepped forward and shook Charlie's hand. They had already shaken hands on the dock back at the military compound.

"Goodbye," said the ensign. It was one of his English words.

"Goodbye," said Charlie. He still didn't know what was going on. Sanchez had suggested earlier that the Cambodians might come around the point in a gunboat and machine-gun them. "They'll blame it on the jets," Sanchez had said. "What'd I tell you, captain," said Sanchez. "They're going to get the guards off first."

No, thought Charlie. Must be a lot of jets out by the island. They want to go back to port where it's safe.

The ensign jumped back into his own boat. "Goodbye," he shouted again. The other fishing boat peeled off to port and started back for Koh Rong Sam Lem.

"Hey, we are free," yelled Harrington. Charlie could see the Thai captain was still jumping up and down. Then he started doing sort of a striptease, unwrapping the sarong he had on in place of pants. When he got the sarong off, he unwrapped his loincloth underneath. Finally, Charlie saw what was going on. Strapped to the Thai captain's balls was a gold wristwatch. He held the watch up for Charlie to see. Then he reached in and pulled out five American twenty-dollar bills. The Thai captain had kept his valuables well hidden.

"Must have been kind of uncomfortable for five months," Harrington said.

Dave English came over to where Charlie and the chief were standing. English didn't seem very taken by the Thai captain's striptease. "What if there are Cambodians still on the ship, Captain?" he asked. "We'd be right back in captivity."

"We'll have to be careful," said Charlie. "Circle the ship a couple of times, I guess." We can worry about that when we get there, he thought. English always expects the worst.

Cliff Harrington was so elated to have the armed guards off the fishing boat he started doing bumps and grinds himself, singing "a pretty girl is like a melody" as he peeled off his shirt. Before they left the dock Charlie had made the crew take off their white shirts, undershirts, and shorts and tie them to bamboo poles which they had found in the military compound. He wanted to have white flags handy to wave at the planes. Omer's mess jacket made the best flag. Cliff was now adding his khaki shirt to the supply of pennants.

At 8:45 Dave English, with his sharp eyes, saw a puff of smoke straight ahead on the horizon. Under it, just a squiggle on the sea's surface, he could see Koh Tang. The puff of smoke he reported hung there motionless. Nobody else could see it. Finally everybody could see Koh Tang and Charlie began peering into the horizon searching for the ship. Then Dave English announced: "There's a Navy destroyer by the ship."

"You're seeing things now," Burt Coombes said. Old Eagle-eye, himself, doesn't see anything, he thought. He'd been scanning the horizon for five minutes trying to pick out a black speck that could be the *Mayaguez.*

"There's a slender silhouette right in back of the *Mayaguez,*" bristled English. "Hell," he said, "I can see another destroyer over to the left."

"Plane!" shouted a voice in the bow. Everybody had been scanning the horizon so hard they had forgotten to watch for jets. Charlie looked up and saw the plane, maybe three or four miles away.

"Prop plane," said English. "She's got one engine feathered." In a minute Charlie could see that his third mate was absolutely right. As the plane came in high off the port bow, he could see that one of the four propellers was stopped.

"Everybody up in the bow," yelled Charlie Miller, "wave those flags." The plane circled and came lower, still staying out of ma-chine-gun range. Everybody waved, even those with only their arms. The plane dropped a thousand feet and made another turn. Everybody waved again. On the next pass the plane flew directly over the fishing boat and waggled its wings.

Commander Jim Messegee was feeling glum. Maybe he'd been up too long. In three days he doubted that he'd sneaked more than eight or nine hours downstairs on his office couch. The rest of the time he'd stayed right there in the OPCON room. But things really looked grim this morning. Surprisingly so. His two Surveillance Birds had been reporting on the TAC Birds all morning. They came in first at 2309 Z to start softening up Koh Tang. Maybe they didn't do enough. His own birds could still see a lot of fifty-calibre coming from the tree line just behind the beach. And the helos really took it on the chin. Knocked KNIFE-31 into the water about 100 feet off the beach. Looked real bad, Messegee had been informed. But his P3 saw some people swimming away. KNIFE-23 got shot down almost in the same place, but crashed on the beach. Had it's tail shot off. All the Marine passengers got out OK, but now they were pinned down. Looked like somebody was going to have to go in there and get them. But that wasn't all. KNIFE-21 dropped off its passengers all right. Then got hit taking off and crashed in the water about a mile from the island. After that KNIFE-22 got hit bad enough so it couldn't land. Limped back to Thailand leaking gas with all the passengers still aboard. KNIFE-32 got hit too. At least they got the passengers off. Never did hear if KNIFE-32 made it back to Thailand. Guess I would have heard if they didn't, he thought.

Jim Messegee glanced at his watch: 1010 Hotel time. Time for another cup of coffee, he thought. Might make things look a little better, not that he hadn't poured himself a couple of gallons this morning already. He stepped out of the radio shack headed for the percolater on the counter by the wall. He hadn't closed the door yet when he heard one of his Surveillance Birds talking to a destroyer. They had direct voice contact with the *Holt* and *Wilson* this morning.

"There's a gunboat comin' out," he heard the P3 say. Then he heard the P3 revise his estimate. "Looks more like a pleasure craft."

Messegee grabbed the mike. "What kind of pleasure craft?" he asked. One thing that had worried Messegee was the possibility of the Cambodians sending something out to sink the *Mayaguez.* A pleasure craft with a couple of rocket-launchers hidden aboard would be one way to do it. He heard the *Wilson* acknowledge. Then he heard the Destroyer Squadron 23 commander on the *Holt* order the *Wilson* to intercept.

"What kind of a pleasure craft?" he repeated into the mike.

"Dunno, Skipper. Looks like there's a bunch of people out on deck. We're lookin' at 'em now. They're wavin' white flags."

Refugees maybe, Messegee thought "Orientals?" he asked.

"Looks like Orientals, Skipper. We're goin' down now."

The P3 must be making several turns around the boat, Messegee thought. The radio had gone silent.

"They're Caucasians, Skipper," said the radio voice excitedly. "Must be about thirty of them wavin' white flags. I can see 'em real clear. They're all up in the bow."

Commander Mike Rodgers wanted to get a good look at the *Mayaguez.* After all, he and his ship had come pounding down the South China Sea some 1,300 miles just for her. He took the *Wilson* close by the port side of the *Mayaguez* where the *Holt* was tied up. With those big boxes stacked on deck, a container ship has a very unseagoing configuration, he thought. He could see a dozen or so Marines loitering on the deck. Those guys have it pretty soft compared to the men on the beach. Right now down in his own hospital, Petty Officer First Class Donald Pourman, he knew, was having a tough time taking care of the wounds and burns of the thirteen men they had picked out of the water this morning. Some of the wounds looked pretty bad. Mike Rodgers looked up on the fo'c'sle head of the *Mayaguez.* He could see some Navy crewmen trying to rig a bridle. Guess the *Holt*'s getting ready to tow her away from the island, he thought.

"Captain, there's a gunboat coming out from the mainland,"

he heard Jim Hall's voice inform him over the intercom. Hall, he knew, had voice contact with the P3 Orions. And in a couple of seconds, just as he expected, orders came from the Destroyer Squadron 23 commander over on the *Holt* to intercept the gunboat. He glanced at his watch: 9:23.

Commander Rodgers moved the *Wilson* out quickly. I'm not going to haul off and shoot somebody who doesn't show hostile intent, he thought. Even if it is open season on Cambodian gunboats. In five miles he could see the outline of the boat. But he couldn't make out exactly what it was. The *Wilson*'s missile and gunfire radars were already locked onto her, and the guns were out. Then Mike Rodgers heard the P3 revise its estimate.

"Looks more like a pleasure craft," he heard the voice say. Then the voice on the radio got all excited, describing thirty Caucasians whom he said were waving white flags. Rodgers centerlined the guns and moved the *Wilson* in closer to rendezvous with the boat. Through his binoculars he could see twenty-five or thirty people crowded on the foredeck waving white banners. There were five or six more perched on the pilot house. And he thought he saw a couple more hanging off the stern. Looks like more than thirty. Pretty crazy, he thought, but up until two minutes ago I would have bet anything the crew of the *Mayaguez* was on the island. It was so logical, with only 1,500 or 1,600 yards of water separating the ship and the island. If the men weren't on the ship they had to be on the island. "In this strange Cambodian chess game why would Phnom Penh move all their pawns to the mainland?" chess expert Rodgers asked himself. It didn't make sense. Not unless they were going to keep them on the mainland. Anyway, they were here. Mike Rodgers reached for the microphone to the loudspeakers.

Charlie Miller looked at the DDG-7 bearing down on them with her five-inch guns and wondered for a second if the reconnaissance plane might have failed to make contact with the destroyer.

Then he saw the muzzles of the two guns turn away and lock into their center position and he knew everything was going to be all right.

"Are you the crew of the *Mayaguez?*"

The words boomed across the water from loudspeakers on the destroyer.

"Who in hell do they think we are?" yelled Cliff Harrington. Everybody else waved their flags and arms and hollered.

Charlie Miller cupped his hands around his mouth and yelled for permission to come alongside.

"Permission to come alongside" boomed the loudspeakers on the destroyer. The crew of the *Wilson* had lined the deck. Now they clapped and cheered.

The Thai fishing boat *Sinvari* moved up against the guided missile destroyer *Henry B. Wilson.* For a second it appeared that the entire *Mayaguez* crew wanted to scramble up the ladder at the same time.

"Let the captain go first!" shouted Harrington. Captain Miller climbed up the ladder to the deck of the *Wilson.* Cliff Harrington followed behind him. As he went up the ladder, Harrington glanced at his Timex watch. It was seven minutes after ten.

They took Charlie up to the bridge. "Are all of your men here?" Commander Mike Rodgers asked him. "Yes, sir," said Charlie. "They're all safe."

NINETEEN

Changing Course

AT TEN MINUTES PAST TEN President Gerald Ford ushered Premier Joop M. den Uyl and his other Dutch guests out of the State Dining Room and back to the Red Room for liqueurs. Three times during dinner he had gotten up from the table to take telephone calls out in the usher's office: the first at 8:50 from Kissinger (who was supposed to be there at the dinner) with more information about the Cambodian broadcast; the second at 8:55 from Mike Mansfield; the third at 8:57 from Kissinger again to say that the Marines had seized the *Mayaguez*, but the crew was not aboard.

At 10:50 President Ford bid his guests goodnight, and still wearing his tuxedo, headed for Henry Kissinger's office in the west wing. He hadn't really expected that the Marines would find the crew aboard the *Mayaguez*, but there had been no report, either, of the Marines finding any of them on the island. It had been a grueling day: NSC meeting, special meeting with the bipartisan leaders, and the black-tie working dinner for the Dutch premier. He would be glad when the new White House swimming pool was finally built. Construction had finally commenced today. In his own home in Alexandria he had been accustomed to swimming twice a day, in the early morning and after work at night. It relaxed him.

At 10:57, while the president was in Kissinger's office, A-6 Intruders and A-7 Corsairs bombed Ream Airfield, destroying seventeen planes, cratering the runway, and flattening the hangar.

The planes had originally been launched at 8:45, but returned to the carrier after making only passes over the military targets in the Kompong Som area. This time they used TV-directed Walleye smart bombs to demolish their targets.

At 11:08, one minute after Charlie Miller and his crew had boarded the *Henry B. Wilson,* the telephone rang in the Oval Office. It was Secretary Schlesinger. Schlesinger had attended the dinner for the Dutch premier. But now he was back in the Pentagon and he had unbelievable news. Thirty members of the *Mayaguez* crew had been found safe. Not on Koh Tang where the Marines were heavily engaged, but on a fishing boat which had come out from the mainland. The president, who was clutching his pipe in his left hand, thrust his right hand across his desk as if he were prepared to shake hands with everybody in the room. Somehow, though, the original report of the P3 Orion that it had observed about thirty Caucasians on the forward deck of a small boat proceeding out towards the *Wilson,* had been erroneously fed back to the National Military Command Center in the Pentagon as the actual head-count of those rescued. The fact that there were still ten members of the crew to be accounted for, didn't reduce the exuberance of the moment. Finding thirty members of the *Mayaguez* crew was exciting news.

At 11:13 Schlesinger received the corrected head-count. Captain Miller and the thirty-nine crew members of the *Mayaguez* were all safe. At 11:15 he called the president back to pass on the now even more unbelievable news. When President Ford put down the telephone he said: "They're all safe. We got them all. Thank God."

Looking back on this moment the president said: "We had all gone through three days of strain, and of course, it was mounting in its tension. The relief that we received from that news, you know, you just can't understand or believe what a wonderful feeling it was because everything seemed to have worked including getting the final good results.

"Unfortunately, we didn't know of the loss of life of the Marines that had taken place, but the recovery of the crew, I don't know, it just broke the ice.

"We never anticipated it. Having it happen so quickly and so successfully sort of just broke the ice with everyone."

A dozen or so lower level White House aides were huddled in the hall outside the Oval Office. When they heard the astounding news, they broke into cheers and applause. A couple of the aides also broke out cans of cold beer to celebrate.

When the White House aides then heard that the Pentagon had announced the release of the *Mayaguez* crew before the president could do it himself, some of them were outwardly miffed. Said one aide: "The president was the least irritated."

At 11:16, while he was still talking to Schlesinger, President Ford issued the order to cease all offensive military operations and withdraw. At the same time Lt. Colonel Randall W. Austin, the ground commander on Koh Tang, asked for 100 additional Marines to provide security for the withdrawal. Not only had the numerical strength of Cambodians defending the island been greater than expected, but their firepower and tenacity had exceeded expectations too. In addition to three helicopters which had been shot down, one badly damaged helicopter had been unable to unload its Marine passengers and had limped back to Thailand with them still aboard. But the men returned to fight later.

At 11:30 the president returned to the residence to change back into a business suit in preparation for his statement to the press.

All Charlie Miller could think of as he stood facing the young Navy commander on the bridge of the *Henry B. Wilson,* was his pledge to the English-speaker. "When they released us," said Charlie, "I promised to try to stop the planes."

"You're too late, Captain," said Mike Rodgers. "They've already started bombing Kompong Som." The Navy commander informed Charlie that the strikes were being launched from the

Coral Sea. The aircraft carrier was now cruising back and forth only ten miles off Koh Tang.

Commander Rodgers took Charlie to be debriefed. The intelligence officer had an open radio-telephone line, to where Charlie wasn't sure, but to some Navy headquarters ashore. Charlie repeated his pledge to the English-speaker. He explained that the promise he had made had been relayed to the first commander of Kompong Som, who passed it on to the high commander in Phnom Penh.

Then they took Charlie down to the mess. Most of his crew were having lunch. Charlie had a ham and cheese sandwich and told each man to write his name in a notebook which was sent back up to the debriefer so that a complete crew list could be flashed to Washington. Several members of his crew, Charlie was told, were being treated in sick bay. Third Engineer Rappenecker was having the shrapnel wounds in his right leg treated and Second Mate Myregard was having the single wound in his right arm attended to. Many of Captain Miller's men also complained that their eyes still burned from the gas attack on the previous day. Cliff Harrington had heard two distant explosions coming from the mainland as he boarded the *Wilson.* "That's a damn shame they're bombing Kompong Som," he said to Charlie down in the mess. "Those people didn't do us any harm."

After his sandwich, which he washed down with six or seven glasses of lemonade, Charlie went to the sick bay. He wanted to check on his injured men. But when he entered the little hospital he could hardly hold back the tears. A major was sitting there, bandaged from his shoulders all the way down to his hips. He wasn't able to lie down. He told Charlie he was the pilot of a helicopter which had been shot down. Charlie had the impression that about one quarter of the man's back must have been blown away.

Charlie felt embarrassed. He couldn't think of anything to say. "I'm sorry you had to get hurt trying to save me," he said finally.

"Don't worry about me," the major said. "I'll be taken care of."

Another man with bandages from his elbows to his wrists, and more bandages wrapped around his legs from his hips to knees, was there too. He had been badly burned in the helicopter. Charlie apologized to him too. He said the same thing. "Don't worry about us, Captain. We'll be taken care of." It made Charlie feel better. But then someone told him they had "seven Marines on ice" aboard the *Wilson* and Charlie felt sick.

At 11:35 P.M. in Washington, while Charlie Miller was still aboard the *Wilson,* President Gerald Ford was in the White House residence taking off his tuxedo. Quickly, he changed to a business suit, then without thinking stepped back into his tasseled patent leather shoes.

At 11:44 the president was back in the Oval Office. He called Congressman James Rhodes and Senator Hugh Scott to inform them of the crew's miraculous return. At 11:50 the second strike launched from the *Coral Sea* hit the oil storage area in the port of Kompong Som. The attack was carried out in support of the Marines who were still bitterly engaged on Koh Tang. (Later this final raid was severely criticized as "overreaction" by many Americans. It was defended by government officials, on grounds that the Cambodians were believed to have 2,400 troops, light planes, and boats in the area, which presumably could have been used against the Marines on Koh Tang.)

At 12:27 A.M. the president appeared on the podium in the White House briefing room to make a statement. Speaking to the country, most of which had gone to bed, he said: "At my direction the United States forces tonight boarded the American merchant ship *Mayaguez* and landed at the island of Koh Tang for the purpose of rescuing the crew and the ship, which had been illegally seized by Cambodian forces. They also conducted supporting strikes against nearby military installations. I have now received information that the vessel has been recovered intact and the entire crew has been rescued. The forces that have successfully accomplished this mission are still under hostile fire, but are preparing to disengage. I wish to express my deep appreciation and that of the entire nation to the units and the men for their valor and their sacrifice."

At 12:33 the president returned to the residence. His doctor, William Lukash, was waiting to look at him. He handed the president a sleeping pill and Ford took it. He also took one last telephone call from the secretary of defense who was at the National Military Command Center in the Pentagon, still dressed in his tuxedo. It was 1 A.M. when the president finally got to bed. At this moment the first Marines were being evacuated from Koh Tang.

Commander Bob Peterson had been so busy with the *Mayaguez* he had hardly paid any attention to the fishing boat with the white flags way over on the horizon. He hadn't been paying much attention to the island either, although the gunfire and explosions had continued unabated. Peterson had one job on his mind: getting the *Mayaguez* under tow. Ordinarily he would have used the container ship's anchor chain for keeping the tow line down in the water and not allowing it to go taut. But the Marine Sea Command crew which had been put aboard the *Mayaguez* still hadn't discovered the secret for starting up the antique plant. So the generators were dead and there was no power to raise the anchor. Anyway, the demolition crew would finally earn their day's pay. Since they hadn't found any bombs or booby traps to deactivate, at least they could use their torches to cut the anchor chain. They couldn't do it yet. His work gang from the *Holt* was still rigging the towing bridle on the *Mayaguez*'s bow. Peterson wanted to get everything rigged and the tow line hooked up while the *Holt* was still moored alongside.

At 10:15 Peterson let go the lines to the *Mayaguez*. A minute later he was backing away easily while his Navy men up on the *Mayaguez* passed the tow line through the bridle. It was slow work.

For twenty minutes or so he kept on backing away. At 10:40 he began moving slowly ahead. Using the bridge-to-bridge VHF phones, he called over to the *Mayaguez* to cut the anchor chain. By 10:45 he finally had the *Mayaguez* in tow, pulling her into the gulf at three knots.

At 12:05 P.M. as the *Wilson*'s gig approached the *Mayaguez*, the container ship was under tow. Cliff Harrington was just rarin' to climb aboard, start up his plant, and get going. As a matter of fact, over on the *Wilson*, he had introduced himself to some of the Navy officers: "My name is Harrington," he said. "I'm the chief engineer of the *Mayaguez*. I understand you got a bunch of Marine Sea Command fellas over there and I know they're going to have a hell of a time starting up that plant because you need to use a lot of little tricks on that old ship." So Harrington had taken eight members of the Black Gang, and along with the captain and second mate, had gone over on the first trip with the gig.

As the gig came up to the familiar black hull, Charlie Miller could see that the pilot ladder, which had been dropped over the side on Monday for the armed boarders, was still there. A couple of the Black Gang jumped for the ladder.

"I'll be the first one to go back on board the ship," Charlie Miller said. As he climbed the wooden rungs, the smell of tear gas was still pungent. Charlie stopped briefly in his cabin on the way to the bridge. The door had been broken open. The $5,000 which had been sitting in the bottom of the open safe, was gone, but the $11,953 which he had hidden under the drawer in his bunk, was still there. He continued on up to the pilot house. Another captain, Clinton H. Harriman of the U.S.N.S. *Greenville Victory*, was in command. Charlie shook hands and took over. There were still fifteen Marines and six Navy men on board, in addition to the five other Military Sea Command men Captain Harriman had brought with him.

While the *Harold E. Holt* pulled the *Mayaguez* away from Koh

Tang, Charlie could see the smoke of battle hanging over the island, where Marine Lt. Colonel Randall W. Austin had now been informed that his only remaining mission was to disengage. The forty captive crewmen he had come to free, he was told, were already back on their ship. Austin and his Marines had found the Cambodian defenders of Koh Tang to be more numerous and tenacious than they expected. There were between 150 and 200 well-armed men battling against the Marines, sometimes at such close quarters that enemy grenades could be fielded like hot grounders and hurled back before they exploded. Austin had called for 100 Marine reserves to help get his men out.

Charlie was up in the pilot house when he heard the explosion. He glanced over at Koh Tang and saw a black mushroom cloud rising over the island. Looks like they dropped an atom bomb, he thought. And it practically was. A C-130 Hercules had just dropped the BLU82, a 15,000-pound bomb and the biggest non-nuclear explosive in the U.S. arsenal, designed to clear helicopter landing zones. The helos had been taking such heavy ground fire, it was decided to really clear a swath before more helos flew in with reserves.

At 7:45, only five minutes past his usual time, the president was in the Oval Office starting his day's work.

At 9:50 Secretary Kissinger arrived in preparation for the shah of Iran's visit that morning. Five minutes later General Brent Scowcroft came into the Oval Office. "Mr. President," he said. "We are reasonably sure that all the Marines got out." He still had no count of the casualties. In fact, as it turned out, it would be five days before an accurate casualty count was completed. (The final count was fifteen killed in action, three missing in action and presumed dead, and fifty wounded in action. In addition there were the twenty-three airmen who had been killed in the helicopter crash on their way to Utapao for the Mayaguez operation.) General Scowcroft also informed the president that the destroyers

Wilson and *Holt* were continuing to cruise the island, using bull-horns to alert any Marines who might be stranded on the beach, to try and evacuate.

At 10:30 President Ford greeted the shah of Iran on the south lawn of the White House. The president appeared unusually somber. Neither he nor the shah mentioned the military action in Cambodia. It was another day and there were other matters for the president of the United States to attend to.

Looking back on his four days of *Mayaguez* involvement, the president felt that it was a turning point in his presidency. He described it this way:

"Although we were successful in the evacuation of Phnom Penh and Saigon, it was sort of a subdued feeling that we had accomplished something in those two instances, but to have an affirmative action go right, gave me a great sense of confidence. It did not only ignite confidence in the White House, among the people here, it had an electrifying reaction as far as the American people were concerned. It was a spark that set off a whole new sense of confidence for them too. We had all gone through a very, very difficult eight months. This sort of turned the corner and changed the course."

At 3:40 Thursday, the chief called the bridge to tell Charlie he now had enough power to give him a slow bell. "Cut the tow line," Charlie ordered. A Navy man on the fo'c'sle head of the *Mayaguez* chopped the thick hawser with an axe. The *Holt,* free of her tow, headed back for Koh Tang to help extract Marines.

"Slow ahead," Charlie Miller called out to Burt Coombes. Charlie stared down at the white paint drippings on Burt's Hush Puppies. Then he glanced back at the island. He could see the *Henry B. Wilson* lashing out with both five-inch guns at the beach on Koh Tang where he and the crew had spent Tuesday night. Up above he could see the jets doing their aerial ballet—diving, climbing, banking, and swooping—firing their rockets and laying down white smoke. Just like yesterday, he thought. Only this wasn't harassing fire. This was to kill. There are men over there dying, Charlie thought. For me.

He was tired. His eyes were red. And the tears rolled down his face.